Johann Gutenberg
and the Invention of Printing

Johann Gutenberg, from a life-size portrait believed to have been painted shortly after the printer's death. (New York Public Library)

A FRANKLIN WATTS BIOGRAPHY

JOHANN GUTENBERG
and the Invention of Printing

by BRAYTON HARRIS

1972
Franklin Watts, Inc.
845 Third Avenue
New York, N.Y. 10022

For Jenny and K.P.

SBN 531-00967-X
Copyright © 1972 by Franklin Watts, Inc.
Library of Congress Catalog Card Number: 73-150377
Manufactured in the United States of America

6 5 4 3 2

Contents

Author's Foreword

Toward the end of the nineteenth century, it became popular in some circles to debase the idea that Johann Gutenberg was the true inventor of printing. This was often simply a frivolous demonstration of personal animosity between rival scholars but served nonetheless to prejudice the position of succeeding generations of historians. To discredit Gutenberg, various theories were evolved—without factual substantiation—in attempts to prove that some other man had actually perfected the art of printing a number of years before Gutenberg had produced his own finished work. It was generally conceded that a man called Gutenberg had been in the printing business at about the time printing appeared on the European scene—but the anti-Gutenberg faction even had an explanation for this. They conjured up an interesting tale involving the theft of certain basic materials from the shop of the "real" inventor, materials which later came into Gutenberg's hands and gave him his start.

In many respects, these theories—which will be ex-

amined later in some detail—were so insubstantial as to
be ludicrous. But, ludicrous or not, these theories enjoyed the support of some highly influential scholars.
They were so widely published that it will probably
take another fifty years before all the erroneous ac-
counts of the invention of printing have been corrected.
For example, all relative material (under the heading
"Typography") in the supposedly authoritative 9th,
10th, and 11th editions (1888–1912) of the *Encyclopedia Britannica* was written by the bibliographer J. H.
Hessels—a man now recognized as among the most fa-
natic of Gutenberg detractors.

In retrospect, it is not difficult to see how it was that
many of these theories could have arisen and could
have been given such credence by respectable scholars.
We must acknowledge an almost complete lack of definitive information about the origins of printing. The inventor kept no diary detailing his day-by-day triumphs
and failures. There were no newspapers or magazines to
give permanence to events which may have been public
knowledge. And, most significantly, the art and practice
of printing—like any other craft of the fifteenth century
—was carried on with some secrecy lest a commercial
advantage be lost to "outsiders."

Virtually all that is known about Gutenberg rests in
evidence contained in surviving fragments of his work;
in some isolated and vague comments appearing in the
works of other, later, printers; and in references found in
twenty-three legal documents of one sort or another,
many of which merely list his name as a party to a trans-
action. This is fragile material upon which to build a
firm story of the invention of so great and important an
art as that of printing.

But fragile, indeed, is any material committed to a piece of paper or parchment unless it has been given appropriate protection against such natural enemies as fire, water, insects, and the insensibilities of man. The amazing thing is not that so few examples of Gutenberg's work have survived, or that his name appears in so few official records—but that there is anything at all remaining today, more than five hundred years later. The city of Mainz, where Gutenberg produced his most significant work during the approximate period 1448–58, was thoroughly sacked and burned in a local war in 1462. Mainz was later washed with the ebb and flow of the terrible Thirty Years War (1618–48), scarred by the enthusiasms of the French Revolution (1793), and further buffeted in the fighting of two world wars. The town records of Strasbourg, where Gutenberg lived and worked for at least fourteen years, were burned in 1793 and 1870. In one instance, this incineration was the result of a sincere (and to the historian, frightening) effort to rid the town archives of the "unnecessary burden" of ancient and therefore "useless" material. A number of significant Gutenberg documents are known to have been destroyed in this fashion, a memory of which exists today only because of references or copies made by early Gutenberg scholars. As might be expected, errors in some of these were built in, and acceptance of the authenticity of any is not helped by the fact that some overzealous Gutenberg supporters, in years past, are known to have undertaken the forgery of documents in favor of their candidate.

Compounding the problem for any serious scholar who wishes to search for authentic Gutenberg material in the archival flotsam of the fifteenth century are such factors as the obsolete and difficult language in which they are written, and the many variant spellings and forms in which the name of the inventor appears. His given name may be rendered as Henchen, Hengin, Henne, Henn, Hans, and Hannse, as well as the more familiar Johann. The variations in his surname are even greater—not only in the spelling, but because of the fact that at various times he was known by two quite different names: Gutenberg and Gensfleisch.

Gensfleisch was actually his family name, and today, after centuries of speculation, it is not really known why he usually chose to use the name Gutenberg. One theory frequently advanced was that Gutenberg was his mother's maiden name, and that she was the last surviving member of her family. According to German custom —so the story goes—one of her children could be permitted to take her family name so that it would not die out. This would seem plausible enough, and Johann, as the second son, would be the appropriate member of the family to carry on her name. However, since his mother's name (as determined by later scholars) was Else Wirich, this theory must now persist as another of those romantic tales of history which bend the truth in pleasant fashion and will probably never be laid completely to rest.

The most logical explanation for the use of the name Gutenberg seems to be in connection with the name of the house where he was born. This was a large family home in Mainz, which had belonged for some years to his father and was known locally as Gutenberg Hof (meaning the "house of the good mountain"). The Gensfleische were a numerous breed, with many of Johann's

uncles and cousins living in the region, and the name
Johann (John) was even more common then than it is
today. It may well have been that the change of name
was simply a practical matter of identification. It was an
accepted practice in the Middle Ages for a man to take
as a surname the name of a place or an estate—as evidenced by the many names in use today which are pref-
aced by a "Von" or a "d'," meaning, literally, "from"
such and such a place. Whatever the reason for adop-
tion of the name Gutenberg, the records of the time
show little consistency in its use. To further compound
the confusion for the researcher, it was a common practice, in official records, to drop the surname altogether
and refer to the inventor in some such fasion as "Johann,
brother of Friele."

Obviously, the Gutenberg researcher needs detailed
technical preparation before he can even begin to recognize valid references to the master printer of Mainz.
Too many so-called scholars have been singularly ill
equipped for this task, which, unfortunately, has not de-
terred them from making their self-appointed rounds in
the musty vaults of history. For example, the previously
mentioned Hessels, in spite of a limited knowledge of
Latin, French, and German, and a complete ignorance
of medieval Alsatian, freely mistranslated a number of
important documents. His biased and inaccurate version
of one particularly important text was the only English
translation for a period of some fifty years and quite naturally had significant influence on other scholars.

Recent and dispassionate scholarship has resolved
many former areas of doubt surrounding the invention
and inventor of printing. The subject was given a thera-

peutic shot in the arm a few years ago during prepara-
tions for the celebration of the 500th anniversary of
printing. A date for the actual invention, arbitrarily chosen several centuries ago and fixed at 1440, is possibly in
error by a few years. But not significantly so.

In reexamining all that was known about Gutenberg
and other early printers, scholars were able to redefine
certain assumptions, to discard certain prejudices, and
to offer new evidence and new theories to fill in some of
the gaps in the body of Gutenberg literature. They went
back, wherever possible, to the original sources and
made new translations, discovering some perversions of
fact which had gone unchallenged for many years.
These efforts have been of unquestioned value, and the
published findings are frequently as interesting as a
good detective story.

However, writers on the subject have tended to focus
all attention upon the technical details of the development of printing, devoting hundreds of pages to such
things as the bibliographic minutiae which establish
that a particular work was the product of Gutenberg's
press. This is interesting material, vital to any study of
the invention of printing or of Gutenberg's central role
in that invention. But the approach of the bibliographic
specialist does not place Gutenberg, the man, in the
context of his times. It presents nothing about the influences which played an important part in the shaping of
his character; nothing of the daily life which he would
have led, as a member of a particular social class in a
particular city in a particular time in history; nothing of
the local political squabbles which erupted from time to
time and which at times directly influenced his life and

his work. As a result, we have a literature of typography, with biography limited to essential identifiable chronology. All of the sociological and psychological elements have been excluded. And this, the present writer thinks, is unfortunate.

We do not know what Gutenberg looked like. No authentic portraits of him exist, and, indeed, it is possible that no contemporary portrait was ever made. In his own time, the importance of his work was little recognized outside of a small circle of men, and they were too busy to bother "immortalizing" a man who—in most cases—was a competitor.

So let us then present this book as a portrait—a study, if the reader will—of a dynamic man living in a dynamic period in the history of mankind. A period when ideas became the chief commodity of civilization, and the invention of one Johann Gutenberg was to become the means by which those ideas would be communicated throughout the known world.

Here, then, is that portrait—and the achievement—of Johann Gutenberg.

BRAYTON HARRIS
Philadelphia, Pa.

Prologue

Johann Gutenberg was born in the city of Mainz, Germany, sometime between the years 1394 and 1399. He was the third child of Friele Gensfleisch and his second wife, Else Wirich. Johann's father was a member of the aristocracy and served as one of the four master accountants of the city of Mainz. Johann's mother was not of noble birth, but, as the daughter of a wealthy merchant, had some standing in the community.

Beyond these few facts, little is known of the early life of the man who has been ranked with Columbus, Luther, and Copernicus as a boundary stone marking the end of the Middle Ages. The early life of Johann Gutenberg is shrouded in the mists of history; and yet, he was a man of his times. He lived in a certain place, occupied a certain social position, lived through certain events. A great deal is known about these things, and, by extension, we can know a great deal about the young Gutenberg, his family, and his friends.

CHAPTER ONE

The Average Man in the Middle Ages

The average man of fourteenth-century Europe was mired in poverty, devoid of spirit, oppressed by high taxes, and too weak to act, as an individual, in his own behalf. The average man could only function as part of some larger corporation—a trade guild, a city group, a religious order. The average man lacked self-confidence; his life was so hard and his vision so narrow that he had little sense of the joy of living. Nor did he have much hope for the future, either in this world or in the world beyond the grave, the terrors of which were made very real to him in the folk literature and religious teachings of the day.

The average man had only a dim picture of his own cultural and historical heritage. Myth and legend were his main sources of information about the past, and while a few serious scholars tried to develop useful historical material, their methods were frequently naïve and often inaccurate. For example, one early medieval historian, attempting to write a complete series of biog-

1

raphies of the bishops of a certain jurisdiction, described his method as follows:

> Where I have not found any history of any of
> these bishops, and have not been able by conversa-
> tion with aged men, or inspection of the monu-
> ments, or from any other authentic source, to ob-
> tain information concerning them, in such a case, in
> order that there might not be a break in the series,
> I have composed the life myself, with the help of
> God and the prayers of the brethren.

In another instance, the whole early history of a city
in Belgium rests upon a series of visions that appeared
to a twelfth-century church official, who afterward dic-
tated the material he had thus received into the cathedral record.

Few ordinary men knew anything about the world in
which they lived, and few efforts were made to correct
this deficiency. In the fourteenth century, there was an
almost complete lack of original scientific investigation.
Scientists—such as there were—would glibly acknowledge the vital importance of personal experience and
observation and then proceed to copy most of their own
"observations" from folk legend or clumsy translations of
the classical authors. The Church, which enjoyed a vir-
tual monopoly in all aspects of human endeavor and
was organized more as a giant political machine than as
a religious body, was such a dominant and conservative
force that any scientist who was curious enough to ask
questions about the natural world, and aggressive
enough to try to find the answers, was likely to find him-

self in deep trouble. The Church decreed that sufficient answers to any question were contained in the Bible, and that any attempts to discover different answers must therefore be considered as heretical behavior. It made little difference that the Bible of the Middle Ages was an almost hopeless jumble of errors and was not a "true copy"—the Church, secure in its ignorance, even blocked sincere efforts to correct the text.

In the Middle Ages, the most popular form of general literature was the almanac. Belief in astrology was widespread, and horoscopes and weather prophecies were taken quite seriously. Since science had not yet unlocked many of the mysteries of the natural world, much that happened seemed to have a supernatural element. Common phenomena were regarded with fear and trembling: The average man believed that a thunderstorm signaled a high-altitude battle between evil spirits or marked the approach of a horde of giants. Strange effects of light in the sky, or a peculiar massing of a cloud formation, could be interpreted to portend famine, pestilence, or drought. Hardships such as these were very much a part of everyday life, and the accuracy of such predictions was always high enough to perpetuate belief.

Organized scientific research was virtually limited to the efforts of the alchemists to transform base metals into gold and silver. Alchemy was an inexact and somewhat improbable blend of rudimentary chemistry and pagan philosophy, but the idea of being able to make precious metals from lead or iron was so intriguing that some of the greatest minds of the Middle Ages worked to find the magic solution. Even as late as the seven-

teenth century, such distinguished scientists as Robert
Boyle and Isaac Newton were still experimenting with
transmutation.

In this goal, the alchemist never succeeded. The
widespread acceptance of alchemy, however, was an
open invitation for frauds and charlatans to enter the
field. Their methods were less scientific but their approach was more realistic than that of the struggling
alchemist. Where the alchemist would spend hours in
boiling down various substances to extract whatever
residue might remain, the charlatan would spend hours
in practicing his sleight of hand in substituting gold for
lead, that he might extract thereby some financial support from a hard-pressed ruler whose fondest dreams
centered on the possibility of filling his treasury with
mass-produced riches. Such trickery did not always go
undetected, and those who got caught ran the risk of
public execution.

But the investigations of the alchemists—sincere researcher and charlatan alike—produced some very real
and valuable by-products. These include some of the
most common and useful chemicals of today. Antimony,
arsenic, bismuth, phosphorus, alum, borax, ether, lye,
plaster of paris, red lead, and nitric, sulfuric, and hy-
drochloric acids are but a few of the frequently accidental results of their endeavors.

Medical knowledge was even more haphazardly obtained. The practice of medicine was barbaric, and
cultural and religious taboo kept it that way. Members
of the clergy—men who were ideally placed, both geo-
graphically and sociologically, to minister to the physical as well as the spiritual ills of mankind—were offi-

Alchemy and astrology being taught in medieval schools.
(New York Public Library)

cially discouraged from practicing medicine because
"men vowed to religion should not touch those things
which cannot honorably be mentioned in speech." The
study of medicine was carried on in intellectual isolation, and all teachings were based, not upon personal
observation and on-the-job training, but upon pure verbal reasoning, as if a properly presented philosophical
riddle could solve the problem of disease. The Church
had virtually prohibited the study of such a basic subject as anatomy. It was not until the end of the fifteenth
century that a pope was to permit the dissection of a
human corpse for scientific study. On those rare occasions when the actual examination of a cadaver was
conducted—with or without Church approval—the
method was less than ideal from a teaching standpoint.
The professor would stand by the dissecting table and
describe what he saw to his students, who would remain
seated and take notes. Contemporary artists and sculp-
tors such as Leonardo da Vinci, Michelangelo, and
Dürer had a better knowledge of anatomy than did the
doctors.

Surgery—as differentiated from medicine—was not
even considered to be the proper business of a doctor.
Medical students in Paris, for example, were not allowed to follow a surgical course until 1634. The practice of surgery was left to barbers who, unencumbered
by the strictures of formal training, learned their craft
by trial and error. Some of them were to achieve remarkable skill, especially in the treatment of common
battle wounds. Even so, many patients died.

The average man had little contact with, or use for,
doctors. He believed that any sickness could be cured

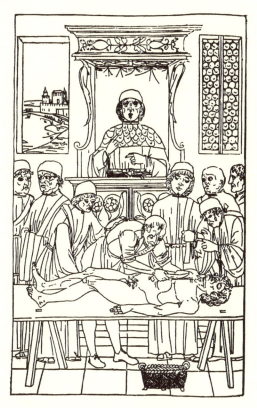

Early print of an anatomical lecture. Professor reads text while barber-surgeon performs actual dissection under the eyes of students. (Burndy Library)

by petitioning the proper saint. Saint Anthony was asked to reduce inflammation of the limbs, Saint Erasmus was asked to ease the pain of a stomach ache, Saint Blasius had special significance for people with stiff necks, and Saint Gumprecht was the man to whom to direct prayers in case of hydrophobia. The intervention of the saints was not limited to human ills—Saint Martin, for example, was considered quite effective in curing sick cattle.

In most cases, petitioning the saints was probably about as good as seeing a doctor. The actual practice of medicine was more or less limited to the prescription of improbable remedies for various ills, the origins of which were not well understood. It was believed, for instance, that toothaches were caused by tiny worms gnawing at the tooth.

The disastrous black death plague, which started in 1347 and continued sporadically for over one hundred years, was variously attributed to evil spirits, or to the influence of a comet which had appeared and seemed to signal the end of the world, or to the intervention of God in an attempt to put an end to the sinfulness of mankind. No one could apprehend the real cause of the plague; no one could discover that it was carried, not by "unwonted blasts of tempestuous winds," but by fleas which were carried by rats which were carried by boat and ship along the water routes of trade into central and northern Europe. No one realized the contribution of man himself to the success of the plague: the filthy cities of Europe, in which trash, garbage, and even the corpses of dead animals were allowed to pile up in the streets. The black death plague brought an unprecedented death rate—as high, in some areas, as 50 percent of the population.

There was no remedy and no cure. The best that the average man could do was to petition a saint—or all of the saints—and hope for the best. One-third of the people who caught the disease did not recover. The wealthy man petitioned the same saints as the average

At bedside of plague-stricken patient, physicians hold consultation. Inspection of blood, sputum, and urine provided main basis of diagnosis. (Burndy Library)

man, but fared somewhat better because his personal habits and family dwellings were somewhat cleaner. But all classes suffered; the plague left deep emotional scars. The world did not come to a flaming end, as some men had predicted, but the occasional return of the disease served to remind man of his sinfulness.

And this was indeed a sobering reminder. The average man of the century took his religion seriously, and it is probable that the visitations of the disease brought the average man closer to his church.

The average man was too personally involved with
his religion to recognize that the Church, often as not,
was using his faith for the greater glory of the Church,
not of God. The Church, with so much power in the
world, had largely become a corrupt business enterprise
run by politicians, with most of the "religion" left to the
lowest levels of the organization, the parish priest, or
the meditating monk.

If the black death favored the wealthy for their sani-
tary habits, the Church favored the wealthy for their
money. The poor man could attend church services,
could send his children to school to learn a few prayers
and hymns, and could count on some official assistance
in atoning for his earthly sins. He could, for instance, receive remission from ordinary sin for a period of 20,000
years by reciting certain prayers before the image of a
certain saint.

In this, the rich man had the advantage. He could afford to make pilgrimages to Rome, to look at the veil of
Saint Veronica (14,000 years' remission) and could
worship in Saint Peter's where, by putting his finger in a
certain hole in a certain stone, he could free his mother
from purgatory. During those periods of time when the
Church was in particular need of funds, the rich man,
by special permission, could be granted these same benefits in exchange for payment in money of the equivalent cost of the journies. Such was the nature of faith
that few people ever questioned the logic of the substi-
tution.

The really rich man, who wanted to ensure his future
through most of eternity, could afford to collect relics.
These were objects which were believed to have had

some direct connection with a holy figure such as a saint or a martyr. In many cases, the authenticity of these objects was certifiable—the finger bone of a departed saint could be passed along with supporting documents. But in other cases, a presumption of doubt, at the very least, might be raised. Is it really possible that one prominent citizen of Germany had a sample of the very earth from which Adam was created? And it would be difficult to resolve the dilemma posed by the claims of four different men to possess the crown of thorns worn by Christ on the day of his Crucifixion.

In the fifteenth century these things were not questioned. If a great and powerful man wanted to believe that he owned a bit of the straw upon which the Christ child lay, who, indeed, was going to question his claim?

But the real hope for the future of one man and of all men lay not in the collection of objects or the value of money, but in the power of ideas. The real saviors of mankind were not the corrupt leaders of the Church, but were the members of a small and determined group of men who began a revolution—the revolution of knowledge.

It began in Italy, about the middle of the fourteenth century, with a rediscovery of the ancient authors—the Greek and Roman scientists, philosophers, and poets who, centuries before the barbarian onslaught, had been engaged in an orderly examination of their world. This rediscovery provoked a thirst for more information, which led to an excited search of all the libraries and monasteries and castles of Europe. Scraps and fragments of forgotten manuscripts were found; the secrets of the Greek language were unearthed from the places where

they had been hidden when the Asiatic hordes had
spilled across Europe and blotted out the light of learning. This was the beginning of a movement, a cause, an
effort, an incitement, which today we call the Renaissance.

And in this burgeoning era of ideas, four men stand
out in sharp and eternal clarity. These were Copernicus,
who shattered the fixed and petty conceptions of the
universe which for centuries had fettered the mind of
man; Columbus, who took Europe out of its narrow geo-
graphical bounds; Martin Luther, an agonized monk
who questioned the power of the corrupt Church and
brought about a revolution of his own; and Johann Gutenberg, who stands as a key figure, not because he offered any original, tradition-shattering ideas, not because he defied authority, but because he provided the
medium by which the ideas and discoveries of all men
might be circulated and given prominence.

Gutenberg was a man of his times. He was not a vi-
sionary, nor a mystic, nor a theoretician. He was a practical man, a businessman, and a product of the society in
which he lived. He shared with the average man the
common beliefs, loyalties, and interests of that society.

But Johann Gutenberg was not the average man.

CHAPTER TWO

Education

By modern standards, the quality of education in the
Middle Ages was poor. But through the twelfth, thirteenth, and fourteenth centuries a system of schools
developed—actually, three independent systems—which
would provide a firm foundation upon which the great
discoveries of the fifteenth century could be placed.

Each of the early school systems was established to
service a particular segment of society, and, from rudimentary beginnings, each was to achieve reasonable
success. The earliest system was that whereby the sons
of the nobility were instructed in the arts and traditions
of medieval chivalry. The schools were held at the cas-
tle; there were, basically, no academic subjects in the
curriculum, but the students were given practical training in the art of combat and were instructed in the chi-
valric ideals of honor, courtly love, and service to the
liege lord. The goal of this system was graduation to the
ranks of knighthood, not the production of scholars. The
system reached its height in the twelfth century and had
more or less disappeared by the sixteenth century. Dur-

ing Gutenberg's lifetime, small groups of nobles clung to their ideals and kept the system alive even though they seemed to realize that their political system was about to be overwhelmed by progress.

The secondary educational system was that in which the sons of tradesmen and craftsmen were given the basic training in their various arts and crafts. This was the "apprentice system," in which a boy was given over to the owner of a shop—a master craftsman—to be supported and trained by him for a number of years. In return for this, the master received the free services of the boy until such time as the boy was sufficiently trained to be advanced to the grade of journeyman. At this time he was qualified to earn wages for his labors. His training did not stop, however, and it was the goal of every journeyman to advance to the rank of master. After this he was considered qualified to run his own business, to hire journeymen of his own, and to undertake the teaching of apprentices.

This craft education was important to the reputation and future success of the community of merchants and was closely regulated by law and custom. The system of apprentice education lasted down through the middle of the nineteenth century, when technological developments brought drastic changes in the crafts and trades and also brought markedly different requirements—both qualitative and quantitative—for the education of workers.

The third and most important of the educational systems was that which had originally been established for the training of young men who intended to enter the Church. Schools grew up at the monasteries and cathedrals throughout Europe, and by the tenth century, the basic elements of a public school system were present although not necessarily promoted. Private schools began to appear shortly thereafter, as qualified teachers were being produced in the church schools. These men would usually move into the larger cities and take as pupils the sons of the wealthier families who could afford to pay for education.

The monastery schools were rudimentary and instruction in the early years was meager. This was limited to reading, writing, music, simple reckoning, rules of conduct, and the mechanics of religious observance. The cathedral schools, located in areas of heavier population, were somewhat more advanced and led to the development of the first universities. This was at first a casual and unplanned outgrowth of the school. A number of students would gather at a particular cathedral to study under a particular teacher of high reputation. This would attract other teachers who would come in and set up their own "chairs," attracting in turn still more students. The term "chair" as applied to a university post had its origin in the most literal sense: The professor would sit in a chair to deliver his lecture, and the students would sit at his feet. Eventually, a school might acquire some stature in the educational community and assume the status of a "university" which was essentially a corporation of students banded together for the purpose of learning. By the time Gutenberg began his primary education, most likely in a small private school, there were forty-four schools in the world accorded the rank of university. Five of them were in Germany.

As the educational system became more formalized,

*A university lecturer at Wittenberg during Gutenberg's time.
(New York Public Library)*

so too did the system of instruction. The basic curriculum was centered on the seven liberal arts, divided into two groups. The trivium included grammar, rhetoric, and logic; the quadrivium was composed of arithmetic, geometry, astronomy, and music. The more advanced schools added instruction in ethics, and in some of the universities, a student could specialize in philosophy, law, or medicine. But the highest course of learning was in theology—the goal toward which all the lower studies were directed. In actual practice, not many students progressed beyond the trivium, and few indeed were those who studied beyond the quadrivium.

The most important of all subjects was grammar. It was so important—and so basic—that the better organized of the early schools were known as grammar schools. Grammar was the foundation for all learning. According to one early educator, it was "the science which teaches us to explain the poets and historians, and the art which qualifies us to speak and write correctly."

The second subject of the trivium, rhetoric, was defined as "the art of using secular discourse effectively in the circumstances of daily life." The highest purpose of the study of rhetoric was to enable the preacher or missionary to put the divine message in eloquent and impressive language, but such practical matters as the techniques of writing letters and legal documents were included.

The trivium was rounded out with the study of logic —the science of understanding which "enables one to unmask falsehood, expose error, formulate argument, and draw accurate conclusions." Thus, it might be stated that the orientation of the trivium was solidly pointed at intrapersonal communication, perhaps the most basic of social needs.

The studies of the quadrivium, while theoretically more advanced, were actually too limited by the general lack of real knowledge about the world to be of much value. Only one subject of the quadrivium—music —was sufficiently well taught and understood to be of any consequence.

Arithmetic was limited to study of the imagined properties of numbers and to simple calculation. But until the thirteenth century and the introduction of the Arabic system of numerals, including the all-important concept of the "number" zero, even the most basic calculations were too clumsy for practical use.

Geometry had some practical aspects, such as instruction in surveying and geography, and included the study of such diverse things as plants and animals. Astronomy, heavily laced with astrology, was too inhibited by the Ptolemaic theories of a flat earth and an earth-centered universe to be of much value except in providing students with information on the method of determining the dates of various holy days and festivals. The Copernican theory, which eventually was to free astronomy from the fetters of primitive superstition, was not published until 1543.

The range of instruction was quite limited. But the methods employed were in many instances surprisingly advanced. If knowledge of the natural sciences was faulty or lacking, a science of education evolved very early, and many of its basic precepts have continued in use down to the present day. Early educators cautioned

NICOLAI CO
PERNICI TORINENSIS
DE REVOLVTIONIBVS ORBI-
um cœlestium, Libri VI.

Habes in hoc opere iam recens nato, & ædito,
studiose lector, Motus stellarum, tam fixarum,
quàm erraticarum, cum ex ueteribus, tum etiam
ex recentibus obseruationibus restitutos: & no-
uis insuper ac admirabilibus hypothesibus or-
natos. Habes etiam Tabulas expeditissimas, ex
quibus eosdem ad quoduis tempus quàm facilli
me calculare poteris. Igitur eme, lege, fruere.

ἀγεωμέτρητος ἰδλὶς εἰσίτω.

Norimbergæ apud Ioh. Petreium,
Anno M. D. XLIII.

I. DE REVOLUTIONIBUS ORBIUM COELESTIUM

The title page of Copernicus' De Revolutionibus, itself a specimen of early printing.

teachers to explain their subject as briefly and simply as possible, so as not to confuse the student.

Medieval educators also suffered from some of the same faults as their modern counterparts. A medieval German chronicler once observed that "some teachers . . . seek not so much to teach as to display their own learning."

An acute shortage of textbooks seriously hampered the progress of education. All books had to be copied by hand, and production—such as it was—was slow and the cost was high. It was normal for only the teacher to have a copy of the text, although wealthier students might have been able to purchase a copy for themselves (often as not, prepared by the teacher and sold by him to augment his income).

Because the books were so scarce, the normal method of instruction was in the form of verbal questions and answers, and the texts were prepared accordingly. The teacher would read a question from the book, and the students would memorize and chant the answer in unison. As an example, the following extract is from the leading grammar textbook of the Middle Ages (Donatus, *Ars Grammatica*).

TEACHER:	PUPILS:
"How many parts of speech are there?"	"Eight."
"What are they?"	"Noun, pronoun, verb, adverb, conjunction, preposition, and interjection."

"What is a noun?"	"A part of speech with case, signifying a body or a thing particularly or commonly."
"How many attributes have nouns?"	"Six."
"What are they?"	"Quality, comparison, gender, number, figure, and case."

This dialogue form remained popular long after the shortage of textbooks was no longer a problem. For example, the famed *New England Primer* was written in this style.

A basic fault of the textbook of the Middle Ages was that it was designed to transmit information, not to stimulate thinking. And, since there was an acute shortage of information to be transmitted, the texts were brief and limited in scope. The total number of modern printed pages which could be made out of the six leading textbooks of the day, covering all the studies in the trivium and quadrivium, would be approximately 628. This is roughly the equivalent of one modern high school text in United States history.

By the end of the fourteenth century, an academic revolution was under way to parallel the overall rebirth of knowledge of the Renaissance. Saracen learning, brought back from the Crusades, had awakened and stimulated new intellectual interests, and the growing body of literature of the rediscovered ancient authors created a unique situation which was to lead directly to the ultimate success of Johann Gutenberg's invention.

In an earlier time, printing would have been an interesting but unimportant novelty with limited commercial potential. By Gutenberg's time, conditions were such that the art of printing could be regarded as the one universally important element of the Renaissance. The printer served not just one branch of science, but all of them; not just one element of society, but all of mankind. Inventors have traditionally been scoffed at, laughed at, even punished for perfecting an item that was somewhat ahead of the times. But if there was ever a right time and a right place for the appearance of a new invention called printing, it was Europe in the middle of the fifteenth century.

CHAPTER THREE

Man and the State, I

Traditionally, the German had been an individualist —a peasant, a hunter, a herdsman, or a farmer. He had tended to remain aloof from community projects and was but dimly aware of any responsibilities which he might have toward his village or his neighbors or his tribe. But, when the barbarian invasions came to Europe, the individualistic German was forced to surrender much of his freedom and accept certain restraints upon his activities. The reason for this was basic: Life became so much of a struggle for survival that the small man could not hope to get along without the assistance and protection of some great man. The great man was able to offer this protection because of the power given to him by the large number of small men banded together under his leadership.

The greatest man of all—in terms of this political system—was the emperor. In the agrarian society of the early Middle Ages, all wealth was based upon the possession of property and, in theory, all land not otherwise legally claimed belonged to the emperor. And this gave

Old print shows a medieval nobleman doing homage to his king by swearing to be his faithful vassal. (New York Public Library)

him a tangible basis for his power. In exchange for a pledge of support from his nobles, the emperor would grant the ownership of a tract of land which became the estate of the noble. In turn, sections of this estate would be granted to lesser nobles who pledged support to their benefactor—and so on, down the line, with each grant being further subdivided among subjects of increasingly lower rank. It is not difficult to imagine the complex titles of ownership which grew out of this practice. There is a record of at least nine different men having title to one piece of ground, it having been passed down the line in exchange for pledges of support. All these men could claim, in varying degree, a share of the profit or crop derived from the tract. All these men could derive benefits from ownership of the land without the necessity of either working it or occupying it. All these men but one—the peasant at the bottom of the social scale.

A tract of land thus exchanged for a pledge was known as a feud, and, logically, this form of political compact has come to be known as the feudal system. Feudal rank—with the emperor at the top—markedly influenced political and social affairs. Below the emperor were the ecclesiastical and temporal princes who exercised control over major sections of his domain. Under the princes came the nobles in various degrees, followed by the freemen, and, finally, the unfree.

The distinctions between the lower classes were sometimes blurred, and it was possible but not common for one of the unfree to have ownership of a piece of land. But in general practice, the break between the free and the unfree was rigid and complete. The unfree had few if any rights, and even as late as the time of Gutenberg, some of them were actually slaves, treated as a piece of property rather than as a human being.

A peasant—a man whose life was centered around his small plot of ground—could be a freeman or a slave by law, but in actual practice had little more freedom than a slave. He was beset with numerous petty oppressions which could make his already difficult life unbearable. His children could be required to do service in the household of his feudal lord, and he himself could be called at any time to perform labor for the lord, for which he received no payment and from which he could obtain no relief even though his own crops might die or rot from lack of attention. Some of the "services" which he might be called upon to perform were such tasks as quieting the frogs in the garden pool while the lord took his afternoon nap, or acting as a human scarecrow to keep animals away from the vegetable plot.

Members of the nobility firmly held the right to move freely through any peasant's fields, often with complete disregard for the crops growing there. The peasant had no hope for redress of any resulting damages, whether he owned the land or not. His taxes—imposed by any or all of several superior jurisdictions—were always high and were in no way related to the actual output of his farm. The financial situation of the peasant was always precarious, and many of the freemen found it necessary to mortgage their farms, pledging future crops in exchange for an immediate—and insignificant—loan.

In theory, all men were equal under the law, but the legal machinery was cumbersome, favored the wealthy, and was concerned with little beyond preserving the

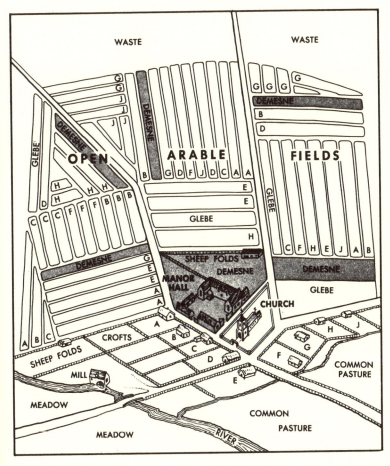

Plan of a typical feudal manor. Lord's residence was in the manor hall.

structure of society. Safety of person or of property was not considered to be of much importance, and although there were some laws relating to these matters, they were virtually unenforceable.

Violence was common—violence from war, violence from sadistic and oppressive nobles, violence from professional criminals or disgruntled neighbors—the people lived with it from day to day. The legal punishments for various petty crimes were also violent—men could be hanged, flogged, publicly mutilated, tweaked with red-hot tongs, or boiled in oil. The violent punishments did little to curb the crimes, and other punishments were frequently so outrageous or presented such impossible conditions that they had no deterrent value whatsoever. For example, the penalty for murdering a Bavarian bishop was to be fined a sum of money equal to the amount of gold which would be required to fill the bishop's cloak; a sum of money which, most likely, could not be found in the whole of Germany and thus represented a meaningless judgment.

In practice, the strongest deterrents to crime were wielded by the Church, which claimed primacy in matters most directly affecting its operations. Sacrilege, perjury, sorcery, blasphemy, usury, heresy, and matters of matrimony were handled by ecclesiastical courts; civil matters in which the Church had an interest were also dealt with. The major weapon of the Church was the threat of excommunication or interdiction, which carried more weight than simple threats of death or dismemberment. An eternity in hell had more terrors than a few minutes of mortal pain.

By the time of Gutenberg's birth, toward the end of

the fourteenth century, a major social and political up-
heaval had begun, which was to eventually wipe out the
power of the feudal lords and impose a reasonably
workable system of laws upon the people. This came
about through the shift in influence from the rural areas
to the new and rapidly growing cities. Feudal rank
began to wither; money replaced land as the base of political power; international trade replaced farming as
the major business activity. Vast cities of as many as
50,000 inhabitants sprang up along the major trade
routes—the highways and the rivers—and the marketplace became the center of business activity.

The pressure of change was great upon all segments
of society, even upon the all-powerful Church, which
eventually revised its long-held attitude against the
lending of money for interest (condemned as "usury")
and permitted banking and finance to become a vital
force in the business community. The feudal lords clung
to their lands and watched their power disappear as
more and more peasants abandoned a life of oppression
and moved to the cities where even a slave—if he could
remain uncaptured within the city walls for a period of
a year and a day—might legally and forever become a
free man. The lesser nobles, the first group to suffer
from the loss of power and prestige, often became va-
grants or petty criminals, or, recognizing the city burghers as the new leaders of the people, accepted positions
as paid soldiers for the protection of the cities.

CHAPTER FOUR

Man and the State, II

The German city of Mainz is situated on rising ground just opposite the spot where the river Main joins the river Rhine. Since the earliest days, even before a transient Roman legion established a fortification on the site in the year 13 B.C., the strategic importance of this location had been recognized. Whoever controlled this watery crossroad could control the movement of troops or of trade along two of the major rivers of Europe; and, in point of fact, the military importance of the city always had an inhibiting effect upon its growth as a center of trade. Mainz never quite achieved the commercial stature which its early city fathers would have sought; at the end of the nineteenth century, the population of the city was probably no greater than it had been at the end of the fourteenth century—roughly 50,000 inhabitants. The less favorably placed neighboring city of Frankfort, 20 miles to the north, was to become the major business center of the area.

In Gutenberg's day, however, Mainz was the most important of the free cities of the middle Rhine district and was an important commerical competitor with Strasbourg and Cologne. It was a principal marketplace for imported luxuries such as salt, pepper, spices, sugar, dyestuff, glass beads, glassware, and perfumes, and it was the major outlet for the products of the local weaving industry. Also, because of its location in the heart of the wine country, where the soil and the climate combine to produce some of the finest grapes in the world, Mainz was heavily involved in the Rhenish wine traffic.

Mainz was a typical German city of the period: The streets were narrow and irregular, lined with huge, many-storied houses wedged closely together. Most of the buildings were made of wood and plaster, with thatched straw roofs; only the churches, the city hall, and the homes of the very wealthy citizens were made of stone. The largest and most important building in town was the towering cathedral which had been built at the end of the tenth century. This was the seat of the powerful archbishop, an ecclesiastical prince who nominally ruled the surrounding area and who was one of the seven most important political figures in Germany.

The unpaved city streets were constantly filled with trash, mud, pools of stagnant water, and the bodies of dead animals. The refuse was removed only for the most special occasions, such as a visit by the emperor. The nearest approach to routine garbage collection was the foraging of the pigs of the town, allowed to run loose in the streets for this very purpose. While the pigs may have been efficient scavengers, they were at the same time a decided safety hazard to any citizen brave enough to walk the streets. As the years passed, and the cities grew, and the city fathers began to recognize and

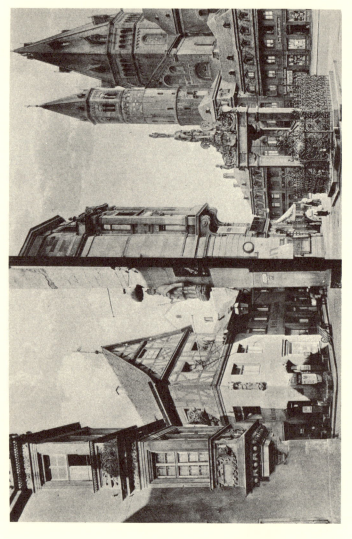

Two views of Mainz showing old quarters of the city. (*New York Public Library*)

accept their responsibilities in government, pigs were among the first residents to be brought under municipal control. In 1397, the city of Frankfort decreed that pigsties would no longer be allowed in the public streets. A few years later, an ordinance was passed in the city of Ulm requiring that all pigs be locked up between the hours of eleven and twelve. Other manifestations of growing civic pride included the dedication of the first public fountain in Zurich, 1430, and the establishment of the first German fire brigade in Frankfort, 1439.

As the importance of the cities grew, and as the wealth of the citizens multiplied, an interesting manifestation of human nature made an appearance—a love of personal display. This was especially true among the upper classes who could afford the curious excesses into which their natural bad taste led them. An apprentice tailor has left a description of some of the things he had been asked to do to what should have been a simple cloak: "Like painters we had to embroider upon them clouds, stars, blue skies, lightning, hail, clasped hands—not to speak of dice, lillies, roses, trees, twigs, stems, crosses, eye-glasses, and countless other foolish things." Another observer of the scene wrote that "the lords and knights think of nothing save making their long hair curly and blond; they try to imitate women in clothing, voice and gait; put on jewelry, and tear out the hair of their beards."

The clothing was nothing short of outlandish. Colors were freely mixed, patchwork style, and the length of the points of men's shoes became so great that one town council felt impelled to issue an ordinance limiting the length to two inches. Another problem arose which required municipal action: It became apparent that the appearance of high social rank could easily be counterfeited by anyone who could make or steal a proper outfit. A number of cities were moved to pass ordinances regulating the dress of each class of society. For instance, in Frankfort in 1453, servants and apprentices were not allowed to wear "colored shoes with points or beaks," and in another town, only the local authorities were permitted to wear silk, satin, or damask, and no woman could own more than eighteen dresses and eighteen cloaks.

As political power shifted from the landed gentry to the free cities, there was confusion in the lines of political control within the cities. In general, cities had been built upon land and were supported by coincident farmland, and most of this land belonged to the local nobility who could claim some voice in city affairs, especially in the early days. And there were groups of patrician families, not owning land but descended from noble lineage and intent upon preserving their prerogatives, who were often instrumental in organizing the municipal government. Friele Gensfleisch, Johann Gutenburg's father, was one of this group.

But the real power in the cities was to be wielded more and more by the merchants, the tradesmen, the craftsmen, who together controlled most of the commerce and much of the finances of the city. If these groups had remained fragmented, if each had paid attention only to its own business, the rule of the patricians might never have been challenged. But the body of workers had an organization which worked in their favor—an organization of their own making, originally evolved for protection but eventually to become a major political force even down to the present day. This organization was the guild.

Each craft had its guild, embracing all members of the trade banded together for their mutual protection, profit, and assistance. Among the more common guilds found in every city were the masons, shoemakers, harness makers, bakers, smiths, wool combers, tanners, saddlers, spurriers, weavers, goldsmiths, pewterers, carpenters, leather workers, fishmongers, butchers, and barbers. Membership in each guild was regulated by a careful system of training and qualification; the quality of the product or service was regulated by random inspection of samples, which were required to meet certain standards. If they did not, the offending member could be fined, imprisoned, or prevented from plying the trade. Since most of the guilds controlled the distribution of raw materials for the trade, it was almost impossible for a craftsman to work without guild sanction. From a business standpoint, the power of the guilds was almost absolute.

The guilds gained their political power from sheer weight of numbers. Some of the individual guilds were quite large, having seven or eight hundred members; some larger cities had as many as one hundred different guilds. Obviously, a large number of citizens could be rallied behind any cause espoused by the guild leadership.

The apprentice system of education was the primary mainstay of the guild and as such was subject to constant scrutiny and regulation. When a boy had been assigned to a master craftsman for his period of apprenticeship, he not only became a worker but was also, in effect, a member of the household. The master was responsible not only for teaching a craft, but was charged with the responsibility of guiding the moral and spiritual life of the boy as well.

The master was by no means given a license for complete and unscrupulous domination of the apprentice, although abuses did occur, and many volumes of adventure fiction have been written with the "runaway apprentice" as the earnest young hero. In actual practice, if there had been too many runaway apprentices and too many sadistic masters, a trade would never have flourished. To have permitted such a situation would have been commercial suicide for any guild. The life of an apprentice was by no means easy, and he was subject to various punishments of the body and spirit for infractions of shop rules or for failure to attend church or for what today might be called "a bad attitude." But the apprentice of today was the master craftsman of tomorrow, and the conscientious tradesman never lost sight of that fact.

When an apprentice was adjudged to have acquired a good working knowledge of the trade, he was advanced to the rank of journeyman and permitted to work, for wages, wherever he might find employment. If, after a reasonable length of time, the apprentice had not shown sufficient signs of progress, it was most likely that he would be given over to another master for instruction at the cost of his first master, upon whom there was a presumption of neglect of his duties as a teacher.

The highest rank in the guild system was that of master. Only he could hire other workers; only he could

Typical guildhalls of the Middle Ages still stand in Ghent, Belgium.

take advantage of the "free" labor of apprentices; and only he was qualified to teach them. In order to achieve this rank, the aspirant journeyman had to produce a "masterpiece," that is, to present samples of his work of sufficiently high quality to pass judgment before a group of master craftsmen.

The term "master" was not limited to the manual arts and crafts; a master was anyone qualified to teach others in his speciality. This included the field of education itself, where, in order to qualify as a master, after a prescribed course of study (usually seven years), the student had to deliver his "masterpiece"—a specimen lesson—before a group of senior professors at the university. If this was considered to be of acceptable quality, he was admitted to the circle of men who could be known, in the academic world, as masters.

The guilds had been formed to regulate the various crafts, but they came to regulate the lives of their members as well. "The labor leagues and associations," wrote one contemporary chronicler, "are formed to the end that the whole life of the members may be ordered according to Christian discipline and love." Guilds ran their own hospitals and prisons, held their own courts to pass judgment upon errant members, and established regulations which covered the life of the members virtually from birth to the grave. A fifteenth century decree of one guild required that the wife of a master "must be of honest and lawful birth and of German origin."

All members of the guild were bound together with solemn vows to uphold the regulations and to help less fortunate brothers in time of need. In case of real hardship, monies were made available from the general treasury. At the death of a member, all others were required to pray for the salvation of his soul and were charged with the mutual responsibility of ensuring that his mortal remains received an honorable and decent burial. In time of war, the larger guilds were frequently so strongly organized that they marched together as separate divisions in the army.

Each guild had its patron saint and its private altar in the cathedral; the larger guilds would often build their own chapel. The feeling of "solidarity" was very strong and was carried over from one town to the next. The members of each guild had their secret grip and other private signs of recognition; by making himself known to the guild lodge in a strange town, a member would receive free and generous hospitality.

The guilds were a vital part of the commerce of the cities; and commerce was what made the cities. As trade grew, and as the cities prospered, it became apparent that there was a need for some type of "international" association similar in some respects to a guild, but organized not only to control trade in one small area, but throughout the civilized world. And not only to control trade, but to protect the traders as well. It was all well and good that a guildsman would be welcomed as a guest by his foreign counterparts—it was often worth his life to make the journey and worth his fortune, if any, to attempt to do business outside of his own district.

The early trader who ventured beyond the confines of his own city was faced with almost inconceivable difficulties. He was considered to be fair prey for anyone from highway robbers to high-ranking nobles. Local

laws and local customs had been established for the bet-
terment of local people—it was not uncommon for an
itinerant merchant to be required by law to offer all
his goods for sale to the residents of a small village
through which he must pass en route to a major trade
center. Thus, the villagers would have first pick of his
goods (and often, because of restrictive taxes and penalty clauses, enjoy a price advantage as well). The merchant would then have to try to make his profit from left-
over merchandise in the next town—where the tax
situation was probably no better and "protection" for
foreign businessmen was just as insignificant.

Some of the laws were made to order for conniving
between local officials and local criminals. One of the
most onerous was the "strand law," whereby a ship—
complete with cargo, the personal possessions of the
passengers and crew, and often their persons as well—if
wrecked upon a strange coast, became the property of
the ruler of that land. Under the laws of some regions, it
was not even necessary that a ship be wrecked for its
cargo to be claimed as salvage—if one part of the cargo
fell overboard and was washed up on the shore, the entire cargo was subject to seizure by properly constituted
legal authorities. (Similar laws applied to cargo-carrying
wagons on dry land. If one item fell off, or if the wagon
became stuck in the mud, the whole business could be
confiscated.)

In addition to such legal piracy, the normal grass-
roots variety of pirate was thriving, and methods to
combat the freebooters were virtually nonexistent. The
business of piracy was so profitable that one pirate
leader, when captured in 1401 after a battle with a fleet

from Hamburg, was able to offer to ransom himself and his crew with a gold chain long enough to reach around the city walls. This particular fellow, Hans Stortebeker, enjoyed such a bad reputation that even this fabulous offer was refused by the city fathers and he was sentenced to execution by beheading. Even so, Stortebeker managed one concession: He obtained an agreement that the city would pardon as many of his men as his headless body could run past, immediately after the execution. The story has it that he reached the fifth man in line when the executioner, ill pleased at losing so many victims, tripped him.

It was because of the legal abuses and the illegal impediments to free trade that the first trade associations were formed. Initially, around the beginning of the thirteenth century, these encompassed groups of merchants in distant cities who pledged mutual support and assistance in the furtherance of trade. It was not long, however, before whole cities became members of the associations as the local merchants and governing bodies came to realize the value in such mutual interdependence. The real strength in a league of cities often went beyond considerations of "protection of trade" and might well have been considered to be "control of trade."

The most powerful and significant of the several merchant associations formed in this period was the Hanseatic League, embracing many if not all the major trade cities of northern Europe in the fourteenth century. The Hanseatic League was so extensive and so successful (it actually was an effective force for almost three hundred years) that it functioned as an independent international body, with each member-city often subordinating its interests to the common good. At the peak of its influence—toward the end of the fourteenth century—the Hanseatic League probably numbered more than 100 cities. It began a long and slow decline after the middle of the fifteenth century because of a number of factors: warring factions within the league; a change in the nature and direction of commercial traffic; the appearance of new trade routes into new market areas—into which the German merchants (bound by their agreements with the league or bound by their own shortsightedness) were slow to move, thus losing a large competitive advantage to merchants from other countries. The change was gradual, the impact almost imperceptible when studied year by year; but, by the seventeenth century, the league had been bypassed by progress. Nations now performed the functions formerly left to the cities; and international agreements were not so easily subject to the influences of one city or another. The league stumbled along, a league in name only, until the last of its once vast real-estate holdings were sold in the nineteenth century.

In addition to physical protection at home and abroad, the trade associations and leagues offered trade protection as well by setting standards of quality, weight, and measure for various products handled under their agreements. Some of the methods used to determine the quality of a product might seem unusual when compared with more modern techniques, but were efficient enough and did much to bring about generally uniform standards.

CHAPTER FIVE

Man and the State, III

Politically, the Germany of the Middle Ages consisted of a group of states banded together somewhat loosely under an emperor who also served, because of the prime position of Germany in world affairs, as the titular leader of the "civilized" Western world—the Holy Roman Empire. The office of emperor was elective, not hereditary, and the emperors were chosen by the seven men who each governed one of the separate states. These men were the archbishops of Mainz, Trier, and Cologne, and the temporal princes of Bohemia, Brandenburg, Saxony, and The Palatinate of the Rhine. The elections normally took place in Frankfort (some 20 miles to the north of Mainz), and the home city of Johann Gutenberg was very much in the center of German politics—sometimes violently so.

The emperor of the Holy Roman Empire shared the leadership of the world—sometimes willingly, sometimes not—with the highest ranking religious figure in the empire, the pope. In theory, the emperor would guide the political and international fortunes of his people, while the pope would tend to their spiritual needs. In practice, there was frequently little coordination or cooperation between the two; indeed, it was at times difficult to determine just who in fact was the leader of what. At one particular instance in history—1410—there were three men each claiming the title of emperor and three men each claiming the papacy. It was, for all concerned, quite confusing.

The first of the three "emperors" was Wenceslaus, elected in 1378 as a result of some behind-the-scenes string-pulling by his father (and predecessor), Charles IV. Wenceslaus has been characterized as power-mad, lazy, and a drunk, who eliminated any opposition to his rule by simple assassination; but such is the nature of history, that it is difficult to determine the facts of the matter. He was deposed for various "excesses" (including long absences from his palace, unpopular treaties with France, and the sale of the city of Milan, Italy, to a friend) and was succeeded by a fellow named Rupert in the year 1400. However, he refused to acknowledge that he had been replaced and continued to exercise control over a large part of the empire—primarily the lands of Bohemia, the state of his birth.

Wenceslaus' brother Sigismund was determined that he himself should become emperor and obtained some support toward this end from the governments of Mainz, Strasbourg, and other cities. Rupert tried to raise an army to fight against the archbishop of Mainz, but could not gain any substantial following. He died in 1410. Sigismund managed to win election to the post of emperor over Jobst of Moravia (who would not acknowledge defeat). The three men maneuvered for as much control as

possible, and the secular leadership of the world staggered along for a year of petty bickering and political
paralysis. Jobst died in 1411, and Sigismund assumed
control of the empire—excepting Bohemia, over which
his brother still exercised power.

The matter of the three popes was considerably more
complicated than that of the three contemporaneous
emperors. Much of the confusion came about because of
the occasional dependence of one or another emperor
upon the support of a pope—and vice versa. The end result was a massive schism in the Church, which could
not function under three separate leaders and therefore
almost ceased to function at all. Several attempts were
made to settle this matter—for example, by appointing
a "compromise" pope to reunite the factions—but none
was successful.

Emperor Sigismund made the most significant effort
along these lines by calling an international council to
be held at the city of Constance, in 1414. It was an impressive affair, attended by no less than 33 cardinals,
300 bishops, 50 princes, representatives of thirty-seven
universities from all nations—and a large assortment of
merchants, jugglers, and beggars. In all, some 63,000
people poured into a town that had been built for a
population of 7,000. This tremendous influx of varie-
gated humanity was to put an understandable strain
upon the town—especially since the deliberations were
to last for a number of years.

The council had been summoned to resolve the issue
of the contested papacy, and it busied itself with this
matter. Each of the papal claimants was represented at
the council, and each delegation was treated with equal

respect. It did not take long for the council to determine that the best course of action would be to have all the popes resign and to appoint a new man to the position. This was more easily said than done. Pope John XXIII, who had entered the council thinking himself to be a "favored candidate" to retain the office, agreed to resign if his rivals would do likewise. But John had no intention of resigning and decided that his best course of action would be to leave the council which, he hoped, would be stymied without his presence. In disguise as a servant, riding an old horse, Pope John slipped out of town.

John had not reckoned with the power of the emperor Sigismund. Under his bold leadership, the Council of Constance declared itself to be above the pope and as such was a properly constituted body for the selection of a future pope. To take care of John, the council brought an indictment against him which charged no fewer than fifty-four crimes—most of which could be substantiated. He was accused as a liar, a robber, a poisoner, a pagan; and not the least of his offenses was an alleged attempt to sell the holy skull of John the Baptist to a rich collector. He was pronounced "unworthy, useless, and noxious" and declared to be deposed; he was found, arrested, and imprisoned.

While the council was engaged in deliberating the crimes of John, and before a final decision could be made as to the selection of a successor, another matter was brought before it—a matter which was to be so poorly handled as to set the flames of revolution burning for almost two decades. This was the trial and execution of an outspoken educator, John Huss.

Huss had been agitating for some time about corruption among the clergy and was in strong opposition to the sale of indulgences by the pope—that is, for example, he was against such practices as the taking of money as a substitute for a pilgrimage to Rome. Huss had been excommunicated, but he had a strong and loyal following among the people of his home state, Bohemia. The emperor Sigismund, expecting to someday inherit the crown of Bohemia from his childless brother Wenceslaus, seems to have decided that the Council of Constance would be a good instrument for removing the troublesome Huss. Sigismund summoned Huss to come to Constance and offered him a "safe conduct."

Shortly after Huss arrived in town, he was arrested as a heretic and thrown into a dungeon. Without being given any real opportunity to present a defense, and without any substantial evidence to prove the charges, Huss was brought to trial on a number of charges including one that he had declared the Holy Trinity to actually include four members—Father, Son, Holy Ghost, and John Huss. This was too much for the pious throngs gathered at Constance, and Huss was soon found guilty and burned at the stake.

The accusers had little expected the reaction which was to follow. The friends and followers of John Huss went wild when they heard the news. Government officials in Prague were savagely torn limb from limb by an angry mob, and eventually the whole of Bohemia was plunged into armed rebellion which lasted for eighteen years. This was to have a significant influence upon political events throughout Germany; and it seems almost superfluous to mention that Sigismund, upon his brother's death was not welcomed as ruler of Bohemia.

The council returned to the matter of the papacy. Eventually, three years after it had originally convened, it selected a generally acceptable pope who chose the name Martin V and took office in 1417. One of the three "contesting" popes, Benedict, refused to give up his title and claimed the papacy until his death in 1424. But Benedict lived in France, and his sphere of influence did not seriously interfere with the revitalized administration of the Church.

And so, the business of the council finally completed, the emperor Sigismund slipped out of town, leaving a large debt behind. His creditors had asked that he leave his gold and silver plate with them, as a pledge toward redemption of his debts. Sigismund—a superb politician and a fast talker—convinced them that his linens and tapestries would be just as good a token. And a token they were; he never redeemed them.

Sigismund was continually faced with the problem of debt. His revenues never quite seemed to catch up with his expenditures. A few years after the Council of Constance, when Sigismund had called another international conference at Basel, Switzerland, he had to send on ahead to borrow a pair of shoes before he could make his grand entry into the city. He covered his embarrassment with the pretext that his baggage had been delayed.

CHAPTER SIX

Gutenberg: The Early Years

What was Johann Gutenberg doing during the early years of his life, while some of these historical milestones were being passed?

The year that Frankfort passed the law against building pigsties in the city streets—1397—may well have been the year of his birth. At the time of the death of the great English poet Chaucer (1400), young Johann would have been learning his first nursery rhymes. In the year that the three emperors and three popes were all struggling for dominance, Johann was struggling with his Latin declensions. On the day that Joan of Arc was born, not many miles from his own place of birth, he may well have been lying on his back in the warm midday sun, stealing grapes from the vines on the hillside behind the city of Mainz.

In the year that John Huss was summarily executed, plunging all of neighboring Bohemia into revolution—the same year, incidentally, that Henry V of England defeated the French at Agincourt—Johann was quite probably working at his first job. This would not have been a job in the usual sense, however, because the members of the Gensfleisch family did not exactly have to work for a living. The family owned income-producing property, held city bonds and annuities, and participated in the operation of the city mint.

What sort of job would be open to—and be of interest to—such a young man? In light of his later activities—not only in connection with printing, but in other endeavors as well—it must be assumed that he received early and thorough training in metalworking. And it is also logical to assume that this basic training took place at the city mint. He could not work at the mint as a full-time employee because, as a member of the upper class, he was not eligible for membership in any of the craft guilds which controlled such employment. But as a member of one of the ruling families, he could very well have spent time at the mint taking instruction from the master craftsmen, under the watchful eye of his own relatives. Here he would have learned how to cut steel punches for the making of coin dies and become familiar with the fundamentals of rudimentary metallurgy such as the melting points of various metals, the properties of various alloys, and the techniques of molding and casting. All these skills were important to the development of printing.

As the boy reached manhood—twenty-one, then as now, was the legal age for acceptance as an adult—he was not aloof from the constantly flaring political squabbles in his hometown. His father, Friele Gensfleisch, was an aggressive leader of the patrician faction, and Johann could not help but become involved in local politics. We do not know exactly in what manner he participated: whether he mirrored his father's influence among the younger aristocrats, or whether he merely added his voice to the cause. But it is known that about the year 1428 he went into exile as a result of his political activities.

This exile came about because of a long-standing and constantly growing rivalry between the old ruling families and the new merchant class. In the earlier days of the city, the nobles—who owned most of the property—had little difficulty in governing city affairs. But, as the burghers became more and more numerous—and more prosperous—they demanded an increasingly larger share in the city government. By the first years of the fifteenth century, the burghers and craftsmen, now banded together against the nobles, were sufficiently powerful so their influence could not be overcome by the traditional ruling class.

The basic point of contention between the two groups was "old against new." It was the noble/peasant traditional social structure opposed to the new freedom in the cities, and the desires for the growing middle classes to achieve recognition and obtain a voice in the determination of their own future. This was an important struggle, and it signaled the beginnings of an important change in the sociological orientation of Western civilization.

But on a day-to-day basis, this change—which today might seem like some titanic "struggle of the masses" for identity—was little more than a series of petty squabbles in which pride, not high principle, was the governing factor. As an example of the type of dispute which regularly flared in Mainz, there was an argument in 1420

over which group should have the honor of first wel-
coming the new elector, Conrad III. The patricians, as
the traditional ruling class, claimed that the privilege
was theirs. The burghers, as the more numerous and
certainly more typical of the citizenry and spirit of the
city argued that they should go first. The question was
settled in a rather simple fashion by the patricians, who
slipped out of the city by a side gate and managed to
greet the elector on the road outside of town. The
burghers cried "foul," burned some houses in retalia-
tion, and also forced the passage of a few new laws
pointedly directed against the rights and privileges of
the patricians.

By 1428, the cumulative effect of such petty conflicts
was too great to be tolerated. The patricians had been
forced into a minor role, a role in which they definitely
were not happy, and they were finally moved to action.
There is no record of the particular event which
touched off the exile, and we do not know whether it
was voluntary or involuntary; whether Gutenberg and
his friends were forced to leave the city under threat of
arrest, or whether they left in a move calculated to force
the burghers to acknowledge their value to the city.
Valuable indeed were the patrician families. Whether
the merchant class liked it or not, a large portion of the
revenues for the city came from the older families
whose wealth was in taxable property, not transient income. The absence from the city of a portion of these
taxpayers put a severe dent in the city finances.

So much so, in fact, that in 1430 the city swallowed
its pride and invited the exiles to return. To sweeten the
invitation, a number of important concessions were

made to the patrician class. A new constitution was drawn up for the city government, granting increased rights and privileges to the patrician families. The older families were to be represented in the city government on a ratio of one in three: Patricians were to hold one of the three offices of burgomaster, and one of the three treasurer positions. In the city council, the patricians gained nine seats, to make a total of twelve out of thirty-six members. It was specifically provided that all meetings of the council must be "joint" and that neither faction could hold separate, secret meetings. In all, this constitution gave the patricians a healthy increase in their share of the city government, and it was a definite victory for the exiles.

For his exile, Gutenberg had gone to Strasbourg, about 100 miles to the southwest. His exact occupation at the time of his leaving Mainz is unknown, but he apparently busied himself very soon with personal business activities in which he seems to have enjoyed an immediate success. Within a few short years he had built up a small fortune and was treated with respect by his neighbors in Strasbourg who regarded him as a "young gentleman." He was so successful, in fact, that he did not accept the invitation to return to the city of Mainz until after 1444—over fourteen years after the original grievances had been resolved.

Gutenberg did not, however, sever all connection with Mainz. He held some bonds or property for which that city was obliged to pay him annual rent. By 1434, the payments were 310 guldens in arrears. This was a fortune in itself—enough money to purchase at least three good-sized farms—and the annoyed Gutenberg seized

Central Europe about the time of Johann Gutenberg.

upon an opportunity to force payment. The treasurer of the city of Mainz made the tactical error of journeying to Strasbourg, and Gutenberg had him thrown into debtors' prison. It was Gutenberg's intention to leave him there until he should be ransomed by the payment of the 310 guldens. This may also have been a form of casual revenge on the part of the "young gentleman," for the treasurer of Mainz was also the leader of the opposition party which had been responsible for the exile. Be that as it may, Gutenberg soon withdrew his claim, allowing the treasurer to return to Mainz upon promise that the monies would be paid. Actually, this had not been Gutenberg's idea; he was asked to be lenient by the city fathers of Strasbourg who did not wish to endanger the friendly relations which existed between their city and Mainz. The fact that he allowed the man to go free without immediate payment indicates one important thing about Gutenberg at this time: He was obviously not in need of money, or he could never have been able to forego the payment of such a large sum for an indefinite period. This can be considered to be a reasonable indication that his early business ventures in Strasbourg were highly successful.

Upon his arrival in that city probably at the time of his exile, 1428, he had apparently established himself quickly in the business of cutting and polishing precious and semiprecious stones. There is no evidence to indicate whether or not this was a continuation of an earlier endeavor in Mainz, or whether it was a completely new venture. As another measure of the success of the operation it may be noted that within a few years he had taken on a partner—a local man, Andrew Dritzehen, who wished to learn the trade and was willing and able to pay a sum of money for the privilege.

But it was not too many years before Gutenberg, with this business well established, grew restless and eager to enter a fresh field. He took on another partner in an entirely independent operation which involved the manufacture of mirrors and trinkets specifically intended for sale at a fair scheduled to take place in 1439. This partner was Hans Riffe; but he was more of a silent than an active partner. He advanced money for the purchase of needed supplies, and Gutenberg contributed his technical knowledge and skill.

A glass mirror was a rare novelty in the early fifteenth century, and the secrets of manufacture were known only to a few craftsmen. The mirrors were made by pouring molten tin over a hot glass plate: when this cooled, the tin formed the reflecting surface behind the glass. The mirrors were usually quite small, but were mounted in elaborate frames of cast brass or copper, highly polished.

This business moved along quickly, and soon Gutenberg had allowed Andrew Dritzehen to join this new enterprise, for a payment of some 80 florins. It was not long before a fourth partner was added, although Gutenberg did not really feel that one was needed. However, a friend of his had been looking for some useful position in which to place his younger brother and persuaded Gutenberg that the young master Heilmann would be a valuable addition to the group. He paid Gutenberg the sum of 80 florins, equal to that paid by Dritzehen for his share of the partnership.

The partners busied themselves with the work of

making mirrors and trinkets and had built up a good stock of finished items when they received word that the fair was to be postponed for a year. This was frustrating news; the partners had bent their efforts toward a certain date and had nearly completed the project. Now they were faced with the prospect of having nothing worthwhile to do. At the same time, they were naturally disappointed that their expected profits would be delayed for a year.

While he had been directing the jewelry and mirror-making businesses, Gutenberg apparently had also been engaged in a secret research project of his own. His partners knew of his work, but did not know any of the details; however, so great was their respect for his talents and imagination that they begged him to teach them whatever skills might be necessary for them to help him in this secret work.

Gutenberg was at first reluctant, although he could not deny that his partners were sincerely interested in learning and that they were hard workers who got along well together. It would, indeed, be unfortunate if the partnership were to languish and die for a lack of challenging work. After some deliberation, he agreed to a modification of the partnership agreement, and new papers were drawn up.

This was in 1438. The new agreement provided that, for a five-year period, the partnership would engage in the "exploitation of new ideas," and in return for the payment of certain additional sums of money, the partners would be instructed in "certain arts and undertakings." The specific nature of the "new ideas" and "certain arts" was not described.

Johann Gutenberg was now in his early forties. He was an artisan of talent; he was a good businessman who was able to attract substantial investment; he had good social connections; and he was held in high respect by his associates. In ten years, he had become well established in the community of Strasbourg and there is every evidence that he had enjoyed considerable financial success in his several business ventures.

It can also be inferred that he was a man of high spirit and audacity; he was not afraid to enter into new fields of endeavor, nor was he loath to ask the arrest of a man of high political position if he felt this move was justified. At the same time, he was not a headstrong or unreasonable man. There is ample evidence for this: He graciously withdrew his complaint against the treasurer of Mainz when asked to do so on the understandable grounds that intercity relationships might suffer. Also, it might be noted that when he accepted the fourth partner, Heilmann, into the business, he allowed him an equal share even though approximately one-third of the total output of trinkets had been already finished and placed "in stock."

While little else is known about the man at this point, one intriguing—and largely unexplained—fragment of evidence has come down to us concerning his private life. This is in the form of a breach of promise suit which was brought against him in 1437 by a woman identified as Ennelin zu der Iserin Thüre (Anne of the Iron Gate). Gutenberg was called in to the ecclesiastical court of Strasbourg to answer to this charge, and several witnesses were apparently presented against him. One of these was a shoemaker named Shotten Lawel, and Gu-

tenberg was so incensed by his testimony that he publicly called him "a miserable wretch who lived by cheat-
ing and lying." The shoemaker brought suit against
Gutenberg, charging slander, and in provisional settle-
ment Gutenberg was ordered by the court to pay the
shoemaker 15 guldens until such time as the breach of
promise suit might be settled. Presumably, if Gutenberg
were to win that contest, this money would have to be
returned to him. It is unfortunate that no record of the
final outcome of either suit has survived the ravages of
time; but, whatever the legal decision, it is apparent
that Gutenberg did not marry the lady Anne. She was
still listed as "unmarried" in the Strasbourg town records a few years later. And Gutenberg's reputation in
the community does not seem to have been injured by
this lawsuit.

Gutenberg—apparently living a full, happy, and successful life—had not yet produced any of the work upon
which his lasting fame was to rest. He was fast ap-
proaching middle age, but it was to be another seven
years after this suit before his first known bit of printing
was to appear and another seventeen years before his
most significant work—the famed "Gutenberg Bible"
—was completed. It would seem reasonable to surmise,
however, that it was at this point in his life that he
began to seriously consider the problems of reproducing
the written word by efficient mechanical means. And it
would also seem reasonable to surmise that the "certain
arts and undertakings" which the new partnership was
to explore were his first organized investigations into
the invention which was to shape the course of civilization.

CHAPTER SEVEN

The Invention of Printing, I

By no means was Johann Gutenberg the first man to develop a method of printing. The Chinese, Japanese, and Koreans had all succeeded in this, centuries before Gutenberg's time. In all probability he was not even the first European to do so, for there are scraps of printed materials in existence today which apparently predate the earliest known example of his work. These seem to have been produced in Holland.

But to Gutenberg must still go the credit for the invention of printing. Neither the collective and long-term effort of the printers of Asia, nor the work of the unknown Dutch printer or printers, led to the development of printing as we know it today. Why? Because there were too many problems of organization, production, and technique for which the earlier experimenters could find no solutions. However, it does not take credit away from Gutenberg to acknowledge these earlier efforts, any more than it would take credit from the Wright brothers to note that many men before them had tried to achieve powered airplane flight and that some had come quite close to success.

In order to properly understand Gutenberg's achievement, some of the terminology associated with printing must be explained and also the state of the art itself, such as it was, at the time Gutenberg began his first experiments.

The term "printing" simply means the making of a mark by an impression of one thing upon another. This is most easily seen in the making of a seal in heated wax or soft clay—a practice which can be traced back to Babylonian times. But, more particularly, printing is the making of a copy of a picture or of a group of words by transferring an inked image from the printing materials onto a piece of paper.

For the purposes of this discussion, printing can roughly be subdivided into block printing and typographic printing.

Block printing—the printing of an image from a carved block of wood—was first developed in Asia in about the eighth century. The oldest extant example of block printing is a Buddhist charm, a million copies of which were printed at the order of the Japanese empress Shotoku who reigned from A.D. 748 to 769. The earliest known printed book is the *Diamond Sutra*; the work of a Chinese printer named Wang Chieh, it was dated May 11, 868. The *Diamond Sutra* is not a primitive, "first" effort, but is an example of well-developed skill in printing. It is made up of six sheets of paper of text, each 12 inches high and 30 inches long, pasted together to form a roll with a seventh, shorter piece bearing a woodcut illustration. The only known copy, discovered in the Cave of the Thousand Buddhas near Tun-huang (Kansu Province, China), is now in the possession of the British Museum.

Frontispiece of the Diamond Sutra, earliest known printed book. Chinese, A.D. 868. (New York Public Library)

Block printing is an uncomplicated process, and is taught in modern high school art classes in the form of linoleum-block printing. The technique is simple: The craftsman draws his design on the flat surface of a block of wood (or linoleum mounted on wood). The drawing is made in reverse, because the printing process is necessarily a reversing process. Using sharp knives and chisels, he carves away all the unwanted parts of the block, leaving the lines of the illustration standing in relief. The raised portion is then smeared with ink (in the early days, probably with a solution of oak gall and water) and a sheet of paper is laid over the surface. The upper side of the paper is rubbed with a piece of wood or metal, and this light pressure helps force the transfer of the ink from the wood to the more absorbent paper. The paper—now bearing the inked image—is carefully peeled away from the block, which can then be re-inked for the next copy. In this manner, a large number of copies may be made over a period of time, but with one basic limitation: Each block can be used for only one image, whether it be an illustration, a group of words, or a combination of the two. Block printing is still in use today, primarily by artists who wish to produce limited editions of an original work of art. Linoleum-block printing is popular for making personal greeting cards and is favored by the nonprofessional because the soft linoleum is easier to carve than the hard, close-grained maple or cherry normally used in wood-block printing.

Block printing can also be used for printing text material, but this has never been very popular in the Western world because of the difficulty involved in carving letters on the block. Xylotypography—the technical term for the printing of text material from wooden blocks—was more easily used by the Oriental printers than by the later Europeans, because the physical requirements of the written language were not so exacting. For example, a Chinese pictograph—one symbol—may be the equivalent of a word or even a phrase in a European language. And in a European language, the placement of the symbols is critical, or they will be meaningless; that is to say, the letters must form words, must fit closely together, and must generally line up in an even row. In Chinese, the symbols need have no exacting relationship with each other, as long as they are presented in the proper order (from top to bottom, from right to left) on the finished page.

But even for the Chinese, xylotypographic printing proved cumbersome and time-consuming, and several partially successful attempts were made through the years to develop a typographic printing. As contrasted with block printing, typographic printing is the printing of text materials through the use of independent, movable, and reusable pieces of type. In attempting this, the Chinese enjoyed a minor advantage over their European counterparts in the same way that they had a somewhat easier task in the field of xylotypography; since the alignment of the symbols was not critical, the mechanical problems were simplified. The symbols were easily cast in a sand or clay mold, using porcelain, iron, bronze, or any similar material. The resulting bits of type were mounted on an iron plate, using hot pitch or wax which, when cooled, held the pieces firmly in place during the printing cycle. When the particular job was completed, the adhesive material was softened over a stove, and the type removed and then rearranged in the desired manner for the next page.

If the Chinese enjoyed one advantage, however, their language had a built-in obstacle to typographic printing which proved to be virtually insurmountable. This was the vast number of individual symbols needed to put together even the most elemental series of ideas. There are over 5,000 basic characters in the Chinese language —compared with the 26 letters of the English alphabet. In order to print even a small book in Chinese, many thousands of individual characters would have to be manufactured and then arranged in some sort of file system so that each could be located when needed. Even today, with modern methods of typecasting and handling, the degree of technical sophistication required for such an operation is formidable. In the Middle Ages, it was impossible. Some sporadic attempts were made through the eleventh to the fourteenth centuries, but the art of typographic printing did not flourish and there is no evidence that the Oriental effort ever came to the notice of any early European printer.

Some printing techniques, however, were carried over the trade routes between the Orient and Europe, and by the end of the fourteenth century, block printing was being used in Spain and Germany for the manufacture of playing cards and for the printing of small religious tokens. One might well wonder why it took over eight hundred years for the art of block printing to be carried over a distance of only a few thousand miles. There are two fundamental reasons. First, there was little if any contact between the Orient and Europe until the time of Marco Polo (1254–1324); second, the intervening Muhammadan culture interposed a barrier to the spread of printing. The Muhammadans considered it to be irreligious to duplicate sacred writings, and

they therefore had little use for or interest in any form
of printing. This barrier was broken by the conquests
of Genghis Khan (thirteenth century), and thereafter
the natural flow of ideas, while slow, served to bring
printing into Europe.

Thus, at about the time of Gutenberg's birth, the
techniques of block printing were known in Europe;
and, for many years, some scholars believed that the development of true typographic printing was a simple
and logical outgrowth of block printing. It seemed reasonable enough. Picture the young inventor, faced with
the problem: How to easily print words. He comes
across a block of wood which has been used in the xylotypographic process; he idly fingers the carved surface
and, suddenly, he has the solution. All he has to do is to
cut the block apart, thus separating all the individual
letters, and thenceforth they can be rearranged any
number of times. From this it would be a simple step to
the manufacture of pieces of wooden type.

However, the small bits of wood required would be
fragile, easily chipped and split. A staggering amount of
time, effort, and skill would be needed to carve the
large number of characters—capital letters, lower case,
figures, with a multiplicity of each. Every bit of type
would have to be accurately and consistently sized so
that each piece could be properly aligned in the printing press; and each piece would have to be within a
hairline of the same height. Otherwise, the printing
would be uneven, with some letters not printing at all.

These difficulties all tend to discredit the theory that
Gutenberg started with wood, although one bibliographer at the turn of the last century made a convincing
demonstration that it is possible to make small bits of

Before the invention of movable type, books like this "Poor Man's Bible" may have been printed by cutting the entire page on a wooden block. (Spencer Collection, New York Public Library)

wood type and to print from them. John Eliot Hodgkin hired a craftsman to carve out enough letters to set three lines of type, two inches wide—and from this, he pulled about 3,500 impressions in batches of 300. The type was taken from the form, put back in the typecase, and then reset for each batch. The quality of the printing was acceptable, but, in point of fact, was not quite up to the standard of the earliest known piece of Gutenberg's work. Hodgkin succeeded in proving only that a skilled craftsman, using the most modern tools and techniques available to him, could produce an interesting novelty.

Furthermore, aside from the technical difficulties noted above, there are two rather persuasive arguments against the "wooden type" theory. First is the basic fact (only recently confirmed) that xylotypography was not attempted in Europe until *after* Gutenberg had developed his system of printing and, therefore, Gutenberg would have had no block of wood to "idly finger" and provoke an inspiration to "cut the letters apart." Secondly, Gutenberg was demonstrably a trained and talented metalworker, skilled and practiced in the techniques of reproducing numerous copies of small objects, such as coins and trinkets. It would have been illogical for him to turn to a less familiar—and less efficient—method.

It must be assumed, therefore, that Johann Gutenberg made his earliest experiments in metal and continued with this material throughout his investigations. And it must also be assumed that, whatever the "inspiration" for his system, it was developed as a system, for if any one element were lacking the others would be useless. The three basic elements were the type, the printing press, and the ink—none of which existed in suitable form and each of which had to be perfected by the inventor. The "movable type" was, of course, the heart of the system. Methods of production of type had to be developed, and a number of specific problems had to be solved in this connection. The design and construction of an efficient mechanical system for the reproduction of printed copies—that is, the printing press—was a major step. (Block printing did not use a press; copies were made using the same slow rubbing process that the early Chinese printers used.) And, finally, an ink had to be compounded which would adhere to the surface of the type, transfer smoothly to the surface being printed upon, and dry within a reasonably short time.

Gutenberg must have known from the beginning that he would have to perfect each of these. But it is a long way from "knowing" what is needed and being able to provide it. In spite of the commonly accepted myth that Gutenberg invented printing in a flash and that his first produced work was the masterpiece "Gutenberg Bible," all evidence indicates that he was working with printing for almost ten years before he produced his first known finished sample, and for almost twenty years before the appearance of the famed Bible. It must stand to Gutenberg's everlasting credit that not only did he solve the problems and perfect a system, but that he did it so well and so completely that the techniques and equipment developed by him continued in use, virtually unchanged, for almost four hundred years.

The steps he must have taken can be traced and some of the difficulties that would have faced him along the way can be imagined.

CHAPTER EIGHT

The Invention of Printing, II

Let us assume for a moment that the invention of printing was an orderly step-by-step affair, with clearly defined problems and easily found solutions. This was not really the case, of course, but in so doing some insight can be gained into the process by which Johann Gutenberg evolved his method of printing from movable type.

The first step was to select a style of letter to be used in designing the type. In this, it was only natural that Gutenberg would choose to duplicate the common handwriting of the scribes—those men who spent their days in laboriously copying, by hand, texts and documents. In Germany, the scribe wrote in square, compact style, which was easily translated into metal, because there were no subtle curves to complicate the matter; and, in fact, so easily was this done that in the earliest samples of printing, the letters are hardly distinguishable from good calligraphy.

The letters of the alphabet, plus appropriate figures and punctuation marks, were then each cut in relief on the end of a steel bar which, when hardened, became a

*In a monastic scriptorium of the Middle Ages, a monk copies
a page of manuscript. (Burndy Library)*

punch. This cutting, while delicate, is not as difficult as it might seem to the reader who may not be familiar with metalworking techniques. The outline of the letter is cut using small files and scrapers, and the very hardness of the metal actually assists the punch cutter in his work. It is difficult to make a mistake and accidentally cut away too much material. The punch cutting is done in a slow and careful manner, and even a relatively unskilled cutter may be able to include delicate, seemingly fragile lines in his work. Progress can be checked by blackening the end of the punch with smoke from a candle, then pressing it against a piece of soft paper. This smoked image—crude printing, as it were—serves as a trial proof for the developing letter.

After the punch has been completed and is hardened, it is carefully driven into a piece of brass or copper. These metals are soft enough to take a good impression of the letter, but hard enough to withstand the next step: the casting of the piece of type.

For Johann Gutenberg, this step may well have been the most vexing of all and may have brought about the greatest delay to the overall invention. Gutenberg had to solve two important problems: what material to use in casting the letter, and in what size and shape to cast the type so that it would best be used for printing.

As for the material, a few minutes' reflection will show that no readily available commercial metal has the exact properties needed for the efficient casting of type. If one metal has a low enough melting point to allow for ease in production, it is too soft and too easily damaged during the printing cycle. But, metals which are hard enough to resist damage all have melting points that are

A manuscript Bible of the mid-fifteenth century, showing how closely early printers followed manuscript models. (*Morgan Library*) too high to be practical; and the toughness of these metals also make them unsuitable for casting fine detail, such as hairline serifs on letters. All the hard metals have one or another additional disadvantage: Some are too brittle, some are too porous, most oxidize readily and are easily corroded by chemicals which must be used to clean old ink from the type.

These various defects automatically eliminate lead, tin, zinc, copper, and iron.

Yet there were two alloys, known in Gutenberg's day, which overcome most of these shortcomings—brass and bronze. However, they share one insurmountable problem with all the above metals. They shrink at the moment of passing from the liquid to the solid state. This shrinkage would make it difficult to get pieces of type which would be of consistent dimensions; and, in the long, narrow shape used in making a piece of type, the shrinkage would be most pronounced along the shank. Concave surfaces would not readily line up with each other and would make the type most difficult—if not impossible—to keep in place in the printing form.

Fortunately, not all substances in nature shrink when they are cooled. Water, for example, expands when it freezes. And so do two of the less common metals, antimony and bismuth. Thanks to the efforts of the alchemists, information about this unusual property was available to Gutenberg and thus his problem became centered on finding the right combination of materials which would combine the most wanted properties and suppress the undesirable ones. It was not, however, such a simple matter to do so—it was tedious, time-consuming, and expensive. Hundreds—even thousands—of combinations might have to be tried. And it is known that Gutenberg once paid more than 100 guldens to a goldsmith in Strasbourg for some work in connection with printing. Modern scholars feel that this must have been for assistance in purchasing various supplies and materials which Gutenberg, since he was not a member of a metalworking guild, could not legally purchase by himself.

The eventual combination which proved to be most successful was an alloy of 80 percent lead, 5 percent tin, and 15 percent antimony. This produced a material which had a low melting point and was easy to cast but had reasonable hardness, resisted corrosion, was economical, and did not contract upon cooling. Indeed, this combination was so perfect for the job that it has not changed essentially in over five hundred years.

Before Gutenberg could design a mold in which to cast the letters, he first had to make some determinations as to what size and shape of type body would be most useful. It was obvious that all types must be of the same height (from the bed of the press to the top of the letter) and depth (from the top to the bottom of the printed line). It was also necessary that each letter have a particular width, so that each would fit properly with its neighbors to form words: For example, if all letters were mounted on the same width body, a printed word would look something like this: m i n i m a l.

Another decision which had to be made was the casting of the face itself. Should it be cast separately and soldered or otherwise fastened to the shank of the type, or should the whole be cast as one piece? By casting the faces separately, it would be easy to accommodate the different widths of letter—this advantage would be off-set by the continuing difficulty in squarely aligning the faces on the shanks. And, finally, it was important that the type must be plane-parallel in all dimensions.

The technical problem was to design a mold which would regularly produce pieces of type which would be of proper size and shape; a mold which would be easily adjusted for the different widths of letter; a mold which would have some permanence (unlike sand or clay) and from which the cast type could be removed without damage. It was possible, of course, to have a separate, fixed mold for each letter—but the difficulty in making each one of them precisely compatible with all the others would have staggered the capabilities of any medieval craftsman. And the cost of manufacturing and maintaining the several hundred molds which would be required would virtually shatter any possibility which the printer might have had of making money from his work. Printing would have simply been too expensive to compete with cheap and readily available hand labor.

The design of the type mold has been called by some printing historians the real core of Gutenberg's invention. It is most probably a unique contribution, not duplicated by any Oriental printers (or by the unknown Dutch printer). At about the same time that Gutenberg was perfecting his typecasting technique, the Dutchman had about gone out of business (quite possibly because he did not have an efficient method of casting type) and Korean printers were busily casting bronze characters in sand molds—a technique which they themselves had developed only a few decades earlier.

No model of Gutenberg's type mold exists today.

However, while the methods of type production have changed radically due to the impact of modern technology, the physical characteristics of type have changed very little since Gutenberg first determined them.

The mixing of a suitable ink for use in printing was not nearly so great a problem as that of manufacturing type, and Gutenberg cannot be credited with a unique contribution in this area. Nonetheless, he did develop an ink for use in the printing process which was well suited to the work.

The medieval wood-block printer used a thin, watery ink made from oak gall. It was satisfactory for use on wood, as the grain absorbed the excess water and the color was easily transferred to damp paper. But such an ink was virtually useless for printing from metal type. It was too thin, too wet—and if it did not run off the surface of the letter entirely, it remained in globby little pools.

Gutenberg made his ink using boiled linseed oil as a base, colored with lampblack. This made a tacky, thick substance which could be smoothly applied to the surface of the type. The technique of application was simple: A dollop of ink was placed on a flat surface and then smeared around with a soft leather-covered ball until the bottom of the ball was evenly covered with ink. This was then dabbed onto the surface of the type.

The third major element of Gutenberg's system was the machine that did the actual printing—the press. The requirements for this machine, simply stated, were that it be sturdy and capable of imparting strong but controlled pressure sufficient to force the ink from the type into the fibers of the paper. It had to be easy to operate, so that the pressman would not soon tire and slow down production. And the press had to be of sufficient size that a reasonably sized image area could be printed.

Gutenberg did not have to design a press, as he had had to design a type mold. There were already several kinds of presses in common use which could have been adapted to his needs: a winepress, a cheese press, and a paper-bailing press. These were in many respects quite similar and all operated on a common principle: A large wooden screw, mounted vertically in the crosspieces of the heavy timber frame, could be turned with a bar inserted in any of several holes drilled around its base. This would raise or lower the screw, and with it, a flat, heavy board suspended from the base which would distribute the pressure to the grapes or the cheese or the paper. Although many historians seem to feel that the winepress was Gutenberg's starting point, the fact that the brother of one of his Strasbourg partners was the owner of a local paper mill would suggest that the paper-bailing press, normally used to squeeze water from the pulp sheet, would have been his choice.

The exact kind is, however, immaterial. Certain modifications were made to better suit it for the work of printing: The bed was raised to a waist-high position for easier laying of the type and paper, and a sliding section of bed was installed so that the form and paper could be moved under the pressure board (known as the *platen*) for the impression, then moved back out for easy removal of the printed sheet and the replacing of a fresh one.

The first printing press may not have been very efficient—but it worked so well that very few changes were made in the basic design for almost four hundred

Sketch of a printing press found in Mainz in 1856, which may have belonged to Gutenberg. (Library of Congress)

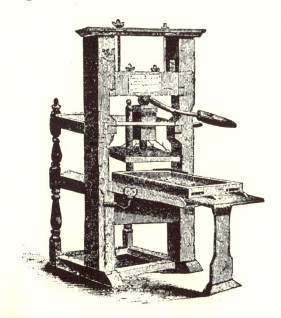

The Blaew Press, an early modification of the Gutenberg Press.

years. The most significant changes during that period were the addition of a *frisket* which protected the unprinted areas of the paper from being soiled, and the modification of the screw arrangement so that the amount of energy required of the operator was reduced. On the early presses, for instance, it took as much effort to release the pressure as to put it on. Later designs had a quick-release feature, and eventually the screw itself was replaced with a mechanical linkage. It was not, however, until the invention of the rotary press in 1848 that Gutenberg's original design was really superseded.

These then, were the problems upon which Gutenberg and his Strasbourg partners were working. It is probable that some progress was made toward solution —probable that the partners spent a busy time in this new endeavor, the mirror and trinket business postponed and perhaps even forgotten in the excitement of the new challenge. But, suddenly, the partnership was faced with a more immediate and serious problem. Andrew Dritzehen, the first man to join with Gutenberg, died. As a result, a lawsuit was brought against the partnership. Andrew's relatives insisted that they either be admitted to the business on full and equal basis or else be refunded the dead partner's share in monies.

Thus, in 1439—two years after the breach of promise suit—Johann Gutenberg once again found himself pleading a case before a court of law.

CHAPTER NINE

The Strasbourg Documents

In the middle of the eighteenth century, the most conspicuous controversy concerning the invention of printing was not over the question, Who? but over the question, Where? The anti-Gutenberg theorists had not yet achieved any degree of critical maturity (in fact, most of them had not yet been born) and it was generally acknowledged that a man called Gutenberg must, indeed, have been the inventor of printing. But in an era of a rising spirit of nationalism, two countries were vying for the honor of being known as the birthplace of printing: Germany, which claimed that Mainz was the proper site, and France, which now included Strasbourg in its borders and which insisted that the vital early work must certainly have been done there. All the known productions of Gutenberg's press had been issued from Mainz, which gave the German city an edge in the competition. But with something of the taint of a Johnny-come-lately, Strasbourg entered claims for the honor on the grounds that Gutenberg's sixteen-year residence in that city covered the formative years of the invention.

Archivists and librarians in both cities were spurred in an effort to locate any materials with the name Gutenberg on them. Since there was a gap of almost twenty years in the documentary evidence of his life and work, it was logical to assume that *some* data must, somewhere, have been recorded. The effort was made not so much in the interest of history as it was in support of local pride and national vanity—but the effort did bear fruit.

For many years, the Strasbourg claim had rested upon nothing more substantial than theory. But then, in 1741, a distinguished scholar and historian published a brief essay announcing the discovery of several documents relating to Gutenberg. Johannes Daniel Schopflin was a man of some skill as a researcher and of generally accepted honesty as a historian. He had been the first scholar to firmly establish the hitherto obscure fact that John Gensfleisch and Johann Gutenberg were one and the same person—a determination that was to be of obvious value to later researchers. In his searches through the town records in Strasbourg, he uncovered several vital bits of information, including some material concerning the release of the treasurer of Mainz in 1434, the breach of promise suit of 1437, and a brief note concerning a civil suit involving Gutenberg and his partners in 1439. There were no specific details on this latter action, only a statement of the judgment of the court—but this was sufficient to whet historical appetites to seek more information.

In the manner of the times, the statement of the judgment of the court carried a brief summary of the events leading up to the action. This mentioned that the partners were to be instructed in, and participate in the

profits from, certain unspecified "arts and undertakings." This was the only reference to the type of business, but to staunch Strasbourg-supporter Schopflin it
was sufficient to cause him to exclaim, "Verily, nothing
hinders us to see in these secret practices the beginnings
of the typographic art."

We may forgive him his enthusiasm; but additional
documents concerning the lawsuit were uncovered a
few years later under circumstances so romantic as to
cause them to be held in suspicion by generations of
bibliographers. In 1745, Schopflin and another man
were inspecting old records in a vault in a medieval
Strasbourg building known as the Pfennig Tower. This
structure, dating from 1331, was badly in need of re-
pairs, and the accumulated trash of the centuries was to
be cleared out to allow the work to begin. The Pfennig
Tower had originally been used as a repository for the
city valuables—the weights and measures, the official
flags and emblems, and various documents and charters.
In later years it had become the resting-place for an ov-
erflow of records from the city hall, which did not have
sufficient storage for a constantly increasing flood of official papers.

The two men were thrilled to discover, lying forgotten in a forgotten room, a batch of records dating from
the Gutenberg era. Knowing of the court action of 1439
because of the previously discovered document, they
centered their attention on the records for that year and
soon uncovered an incomplete rough draft of the testimony of some of the witnesses. This had apparently
been made up by the court clerk as a guide for the preparation of the final smooth copy.

The documents contained a listing of all the witnesses, the testimony of thirteen of the twenty-six who had been called against Gutenberg, and the testimony of three of the fourteen witnesses who had spoken in his favor. A related document recorded the complaint of a suit for slander, wherein Gutenberg's valet had brought an action against one of the plaintiffs for publicly calling him a liar.

Incomplete though they may be, these documents have been of significant value in piecing together the story of Gutenberg and his work. The testimony of the witnesses does in fact contain some direct reference to printing and indirect reference to certain related procedures. This is not to say that they have been fully accepted by all bibliographers—because of a number of reasons, not the least of which are the difficult and obscure language in which they are written and the fact that the original documents are no longer in existence. These were destroyed in several stages between 1793 (a result of the French Revolution) and 1870 (when the city library was burned during a siege). The documents had been examined and copied by a number of scholars over the years, and several inaccurate translations (which were to greatly mislead later investigators) had been made. This, coupled with the fact that the testimony is incomplete and the references to printing reasonably vague, has provoked a string of misinterpretations by various men.

To briefly summarize the significant portions of the testimony: A suit was brought against Gutenberg by George and Nicholas Dritzehen, claiming the right to assume their dead brother's role in the partnership of Gutenberg, Riffe, and Heilmann. If this were not to be granted, then they demanded—as the rightful heirs—that any monies invested by their brother be returned to them. The brothers Dritzehen had first approached Gutenberg directly in this, and both requests had been emphatically denied. And so they presented the issue to be decided by the city council of Strasbourg.

George Dritzehen, who was a minor city official, has been identified by researchers as having been the instigator of at least five lawsuits. His contentious nature seems well established; and, in fact, some seven years after the Gutenberg suit he and his brother were suing each other over Andrew's estate; each accused the other of having stolen Andrew's belongings immediately after his death. Among these belongings were some tools and materials which should properly have been returned to the partnership, but which "disappeared" before Gutenberg could pick them up from Andrew's home.

There was actually little point in the brothers taking this matter to the city council, as the contractual agreements drawn up between the partners had been quite explicit in the matter of the death of any member of the group. A specific clause stipulated that the partners would pay to the heirs of the deceased the sum of 100 florins, five years from the date of the agreement. The Dritzehens knew of the agreement, as they had found a copy of the contract among Andrew's papers; but Andrew had been in failing health (possibly the victim of tuberculosis) and had been unable to sign the contract before his death. The brothers sought to prove that the agreement was therefore null and void.

The witnesses offered by the plaintiffs testified essentially as follows: Andrew Dritzehen had in fact been in-

volved in some type of business venture with Gutenberg
and the others; he had frequently been seen working at
home, late into the night; he at one time had stated that
he had invested almost 500 florins in the business; he
had mortgaged his property and spent his inheritance to
obtain this sum, but he needed still more money. He
was confident, however, that his investment would be
returned within a year.

The witnesses for Gutenberg primarily concerned
themselves with the financial and contractual arrangements of the partnership. The testimony brought out
that the original partnership (for the production of mirrors and trinkets for sale at the fair) had been established on the following basis: Gutenberg held one-half
interest, John Riffe held one-quarter, and Andrew Heilmann and Andrew Dritzehen shared the remaining
quarter. For their share, the two Andrews had paid 80
florins apiece.

When the fair had been postponed and the partnership modified to encompass the secret work of Gutenberg, the two Andrews agreed to pay an additional 125
florins each. A sum of 50 florins was to be paid at once,
and the balance of 75 florins would be paid in three
later installments. The testimony brought out that Andrew Heilmann paid his 50 florins, but that Andrew Dritzehen was only able to pay at that time 40 florins. He
died soon after, and thus, under the agreement, owed
Gutenberg a total of 85 florins.

Since the agreement had included the clause which
called for payment of 100 florins to the heirs of any deceased partner, Gutenberg made a move to ease the judicial process by offering to pay the brothers this sum

immediately after the trial, rather than waiting out the five-year period. He qualified this, however, by stipulating that the 85 florins which Andrew Dritzehen had been in arrears should first be deducted. In other words, Gutenberg would pay to the estate the balance of 15 florins.

The judges thought that this was an equable solution and ordered it executed and accepted by all parties. They ruled that the fact that Andrew had not actually signed the agreement did not invalidate the arrangements proposed therein, as the testimony of numerous witnesses had been sufficient to establish the fact that Andrew had been in complete accord with the proposals.

Thus, the suit was resolved in Gutenberg's favor: he neither had to admit the brothers to the partnership, nor return all the monies which Andrew had invested over the years. The historical value of this action would have been insignificant had it not been for several more or less offhand remarks made during the testimony of some of the witnesses. Although not always clear in meaning, these comments certainly tend to prove that Gutenberg was in fact engaged in work connected with the development of printing.

The most specific reference was made by a goldsmith, John Dunne. He testified that "about three years ago" (that is, in about 1436), he had earned from Gutenberg about 100 florins "solely for that which belonged to printing." This has generally been interpreted to mean that Dunne assisted Gutenberg in obtaining metals for use in the casting of type. Since Gutenberg had previously been engaged in an occupation which required quantities of metal—for mirror frames, and so forth—and since he could not be a member of the goldsmith's guild, he would logically have needed the assistance of a man like Dunne over a period of several years. It is important that Dunne had made definite reference to a particular sum involved with "printing," since it strengthens the conjecture that this was the business over which the suit had been brought to court.

Several witnesses (at least five whose testimony has survived) mentioned that one part of the equipment of the partnership was a "press." Witness Conrad Saspach, identified as a "wood turner," testified that he made the press; and the fact that he was noted to be a "wood turner" rather than the less specialized "carpenter" can be taken as fair evidence that this press was similar to later models in that it would most likely have had a large wooden screw as the principal working part. Another witness stated that the press was kept at the home of Andrew Dritzehen, and that when he died, Gutenberg had apparently been anxious to have the press or some related piece of equipment (the testimony is not clear on this point) disassembled, so that visiting mourners would not "know what it is, for he [Gutenberg] would not like it if anyone saw it."

There has been a long continuing discussion among printing historians as to the exact nature of the equipment which the inventor wanted "disassembled." One of the witnesses had inferred that it was the press itself, but several others referred to some smaller object which was "lying" in the press, which was composed of "four pieces" and which "would fall asunder" with the opening of "two small hand screws." Gutenberg wanted the four pieces arranged on the press in such a manner that "nobody could see or comprehend anything." These "four pieces" have been variously interpreted by scholars to be parts of the press, four pages of type (or wood blocks) in a printing form, or the components of the all-important type mold. This latter explanation was first suggested by the American printing historian Theodore L. De Vinne in his 1876 book, *The Invention of Printing*. De Vinne, who was possibly the first professional printer to delve into the history of the art, brought an invaluable practical knowledge to the subject, and his book remains a classic in the field. Otto Fuhrmann, in *Gutenberg and the Strasbourg Documents of 1439* (published in 1940), expands on De Vinne's thesis and sets forth a most persuasive argument for the pieces having been the type mold.

In this connection, it might be of interest to briefly point out the manner in which some serious errors crept into the text of these documents—errors which compounded the confusion and added to the ambiguity of the incomplete records. Some of the errors were the result of honest misinterpretation, some were the result of an ignorance of the mechanics of the printing process, and some were the result of overzealous national pride. Very few of the men who had an opportunity to examine the documents in the original enjoyed any particular qualifications as scholars.

In the original documents, the key word in the matter of the "four pieces" is the German word *Stücke*—which means, quite literally, "pieces." However, one bibliographer, assuming that the "pieces" were really "pages" of type lying in the bed of the press, rendered this word (in his Latin translation) as *paginas*. Since few bibliographers could read the original Alsatian text, many relied upon this Latin translation—and many, therefore, were led into error. One writer, translating from a German text, was so influenced by the Latin version that he still translated the word as "pages" rather than "pieces." To complicate this particular matter, one translator, believing that these objects were in fact pages of type, used the printer's term "to distribute" (meaning "to return pieces of type to the typecase") whereas the text actually read "to take apart."

It is not only in technical matters that the translators went astray. Otto Fuhrmann, in his book on the documents, most succinctly demonstrates how a simple item —the occupation of one of the witnesses—was progressively misconstrued by various translators. The example refers to Barbara of Zabern, identified as a tradeswoman. (*Die Koufelerin* in the Alsatian text; *die Verkäuferin* in modern German.)

Fuhrmann writes: "Nelson says 'merchant.' As no woman could be an independent merchant in the 15th century, she must have been a small retailer, probably a peddler. Schopflin's (Latin) *taberensis* would be 'servant girl in an inn,' which an American might translate into 'barmaid,' thus getting still further away from 'merchant.' Laborde's (French) *mercière* indicates 'a seller of dry goods and notions'—a peddler's occupation; De Vinne says 'mercer.'

"The diminutive of the name indicates that she was a young person; later on, in the list of witnesses, she is called 'the little maid' (*das clein frowel*). *Zabern* is a town about 30 miles N.W. of Strasbourg; De Vinne mistakes it as a family name and speaks of 'Madame Zabern.' "

However, in spite of the errors, and in spite of a long-questioned authenticity, the importance of the Strasbourg documents is well established and they are now accepted as genuine. The information which they contain, although incomplete and ambiguous, seems sufficient to establish the fact that Gutenberg was in fact engaged in the development of printing, perhaps as early as 1436. This was some twenty years before the appearance of the "Gutenberg Bible" (which is more properly identified as "the 42-line Bible" because Gutenberg may have printed at least one other edition of the Bible, this one containing 36 lines per page and therefore known as the 36-line Bible). This twenty-year period is of particular interest in that it dispels the once commonly held notion that the 42-line Bible was Gutenberg's first printed work.

CHAPTER TEN

The Price of Success

What became of the remaining partnership, after the lawsuit, is not known. It is possible that the business was dissolved. Yet it is from about this time that we can trace a definite change in Gutenberg's fortunes: a change for the worse, even as he continued to perfect his invention.

A few years earlier, he had been well enough off financially to forego the payment of 310 guldens from the city of Mainz; he had been a successful gemstone polisher, as evidenced by the fact that he took on a partner (Andrew Dritzehen) to help him in the business. He had had no difficulty in attracting other men to work in partnership with him in preparing trinkets for sale at the fair and, in fact, he tried to turn away Andrew Heilmann as he apparently did not need another partner—nor did he need Heilmann's investment. Then, when the fair was postponed and the partnership was expanded to cover "other arts," the partners readily agreed to pay an additional sum of money—and a considerable sum, at that— to be instructed in those arts. In all this, we can see Gutenberg as nothing short of successful.

But within a few years, the picture began to change. The constant drain upon his capital to pay for material needed in his experiments began to have a serious effect upon his financial standing. If he kept on with his gemstone business (which seems unlikely) it did not bring in enough money to offset his continuing expenses. He probably did not go through with the plans for the trinket business and may have turned the already finished stock over to his partners. It is most likely that he became caught up in the excitement of his new invention, trapped in visions of his own making, unable to stay away from his experiments when success seemed nearer each day—each week—each year.

By 1442, Gutenberg was badly in need of money. He arranged for a loan of 80 pounds at 5 percent interest from the Saint Thomas Parish at Strasbourg. The charging of interest was still at this time generally forbidden by both canon and civil law (it was not considered proper that money should be used for the making of money), and so the "loan" was recorded in such a fashion that it would appear that Gutenberg had sold an annuity of 4 pounds per year to the Saint Thomas Parish. The selling price, which he received, was 80 pounds. He was thus obligated to pay at least the 4 pounds' interest per year as long as he kept "title" to the 80 pounds.

Two years later, in 1444, another item touching upon his financial position was entered in an official Strasbourg city record. The city was under threat of attack, and the citizens were being mobilized for defense. Gutenberg, as a patrician, was ordered to provide one-half of a horse for the city's forces, and was himself liable for service as a cavalryman. The fact that he was expected

A *fragment of the grammar printed by Donatus. (New York Public Library)*

to contribute only one-half of a horse, while some of his compatriots might be furnishing a whole troop of horses, is fair evidence that his personal fortunes had continued to ebb. This is the last record which touches on his residence in Strasbourg; it is not known whether he left the city at this time or whether he remained for a few more years.

The next known fact about his life also directly relates to his finances. Having returned to Mainz sometime after 1444, he borrowed, in 1448, the sum of 150 guldens (at 5 percent interest) from a relative, Arnold Gelthuss.

During these years (1439–48) he definitely continued his work in printing. It is from this period that we have the first probable samples of his work (although it should be pointed out that his name, as printer, actually appears on none of the pieces attributed to him). The oldest is a fragment of a poem, *World Judgment,* to which has been assigned the approximate date of 1445. Since this fragment was discovered in Mainz (in 1892) it is possible that it was printed in that city.

The next work attributed to his press was a grammar by Donatus, of which he issued three editions dating from about 1446. The style of the type used in these shows some improvement over that of the *World Judgment,* but is sufficiently similar that it can be presumed to be the work of the same printer. For that matter, other evidence—such as the recorded comments of some of his contemporaries—fairly establishes the fact that Gutenberg was the only man in the area doing any printing at all during these years. Thus, the business of attributing work to his press became a matter of prop-

erly determining the date and place of origin of the
printed matter in question. This can be done with reasonable accuracy by studying such indicators as the language, the style of the type used, the kind of ink, the
kind of paper or the grade of parchment used, and so
forth. The content of the item may also be of value in
determining date or place: For example, a fragment of
an astronomical calendar (which incidentally shows further improvements in style and technique over the
"Donatus") has been assigned the date 1447 by compu-
tation of the phases of the moon shown on the calendar.

By 1448, when Gutenberg found it necessary to borrow from his relative, he had produced a number of finished works. The total output is unknown, but there are
a number of surviving fragments that indicate he was
hard at work. There is no indication as to whether or
not he was able to sell his materials, and since he was
obviously in need of money, we must presume that his
income did not match his overhead. The loan of 150
guldens seems to have been of assistance for two years,
but then, in 1450, he was once again in difficulty. Apparently he had made enough progress in the development of his invention to interest a wealthy merchant
of Mainz, John Fust, in granting him a loan of 800 guldens
to be used in setting up a printing establishment. The
equipment in the shop was to stand as security for the
loan.

But even this sum was not sufficient for Gutenberg's
needs, and in 1452, Fust advanced him another 800
guldens. This second sum was not represented as a loan,
but as an investment "for the profit of both." The money
went into new and improved equipment, in the refine-

ment of the type fonts, and in the production of a few printed items.

If Gutenberg had died at this point, or stopped working, he would be known today only as an innovator who discovered some technically interesting processes which proved of value, in later years, to other printers. Or, he may not have been remembered for anything at all, for there may have been no one competent to carry on his work. But Gutenberg did not die and did not stop his work. Indeed, it was during this period that he conceived the idea for the masterwork which has ever since been synonymous with his name—the great Bible.

Sometime in 1454 or 1455, work began on what has long been regarded as perhaps the finest example of the printer's art ever produced anywhere. It is a large book and was issued in two volumes, the Old and New Testaments. The pages are laid out in a double column, with most pages having 42 lines of type per column—hence the usual bookman's designation of this work as "the 42-line Bible." (The more common term, "the Gutenberg Bible," is misleading in that it now seems probable that Gutenberg printed at least one other edition of the Bible, using a 36-line format.) For some unexplained reason, not all the pages have 42 lines; in some copies, the first nine pages carry 40 lines of type and the tenth, 41 lines. Various bibliographers have advanced theories to explain this variance. The theories are interesting, but not very conclusive. One holds that the 42-line format resulted from using a 42-line manuscript Bible as a basic text, and that the irregular pages were either in the original or were accidental. Another theory offers the proposition that the printer started out with

Libr generacōnis ihesu xpi
fili dauid:fili abraham.
Abraham genuit ysaac:
ysaac aut genuit iacob.
Jacob aut genuit iudā et fratres ei9:
iudas aut genuit phares et zara de
thamar. Phares aut genuit esrom:
esrom aut genuit aram. Aram aut
genuit aminadab: aminadab aut genuit naalō. Naasōn aut genuit salo-
mon:salomō aut genuit booz et raab.
Booz aut genuit obeth ex ruth:obeth
aut genuit iesse. Jesse aut genuit dauid regē: dauid autē rex genuit salo-
monē ex ea q fuit urie. Salomō aut
genuit roboam:roboam aut genuit
abyam. Abyas aut genuit asa: asa
aut genuit iosaphat. Josaphat aut
genuit ioram:ioram aut genuit ozi-
am. Ozias autē genuit ioatham: ioatham aut genuit achaz. Achaz autē
genuit ezechiam:ezechias aut genuit
manassen: manasses aut genuit ammon. Ammon aut genuit iosiam:
iosias aut genuit iechoniam et fres ei9
i trāsmigracione babilonis. Et post
transmigracionē babilonis iechonias
genuit salathiel: salathiel aut genuit
zorobabel. Zorobabel aut genuit abi-
ud:abiud autem genuit eliachim. Eliachim aut genuit azor: azor aut genuit sadoch. Sadoch autem genuit a-
chim: achim aut genuit eliud. Eliud
aut genuit eleazar:eleazar aut genuit
mathan. Mathan aut genuit iacob:
iacob aut genuit ioseph uirū marie:
de qua nat9 est ihesus: qui uocatur
xpc. Omnes itaq generaciones ab a-
braham usq ad dauid generacioues
xiiiiordecim: et a dauid usq ad transmigracionē babilonis generaciones
xiiiior: a transmigracione babilonis

usq ad xpm generaciones quatuor-
decim. Xpi autem generacio sic erat.
Cum esset desponsata mater ihesu maria ioseph: ātq cōuenirent inuenta ē
i utero habēs de spiritu sācto. Joseph
autem uir ei9 cū esset iustus et nollet
eam traducere: uoluit occulte dimitte-
re eam:hec aut eo cogitante:ecce āgelus dūi apparuit i somnis ioseph di-
cens. Joseph fili dauid:noli timere ac-
cipere maria cōiugem tuā. Nō eni in
ea natū est: de spiritu sancto est. Pariet aut filiū:et uocabis nomen eius ihe-
sum.Ipse eni saluū faciet ppłm suum
a peccatis eoꝝ. Hoc autem totū factū
est:ut adimpleretur qđ dictū esset a dō-
mino p prophetā dicentem. Ecce uir-
go in utero habebit et pariet filiū:et uo-
cabit nomen eius emanuel: qđ est in-
terpretatū nobiscum deus. Exurgens
aut ioseph a somno fecit sicut pcepit
ei āgelus dūi: et accepit cōiugem suā.
Et non cognoscebat eam donec pepe-
rit filium suum primogenitum: et
uocauit nomen eius ihesum. Ca. ii.

Cum natus esset ihesus in bethleem iude i diebz herodis regis:ec-
ce magi ab oriente uenerūt ierosoli-
mam dicentes. Ubi est qui natus est
rex iudeoꝝ ? Uidimus eni stellā eius
in oriente: et uenim9 adorare eū. Au-
diens autem herodes rex turbatus ē:
et oīs iherosolima cū illo. Et cōgre-
gans omnes principes sacerdotū et
scribas ppłi: sciscitabat ab eis ubi xpc
nasceret. At illi dixerūt ei. In bethleem
iude. Sic eni scriptū est p prophetam.
Et tu bethleem terra iuda: nequaq mi-
nima es i principibs iuda. Et te eni ex-
et dux qui regat ppłm meum israhel.
Tūc herodes clam uocatis magis dili-
genter didicit ab eis tempus stelle q

A page from Gutenberg's 42-line Bible.

40 lines and then discovered that if he followed this format throughout, the book would run to too many pages and become too costly to produce. So he filed down the type and reset for 42 lines. This theory explains the tenth page of 41 lines as a "trial" page which turned out to still have not enough lines for "economy." This theory—while apparently generally accepted—leaves a few questions still unanswered. For example, even the most casual printer will always compute the number of pages and press forms needed before he ever begins production—and Gutenberg was far from casual in his work. Also, by running a 40-line format throughout, the book would have been, perhaps, no more than 60 pages longer than as issued. Since the finished Bible has 1,282 pages, produced with obvious attention to detail and without any attempt at production econo-mies, it is difficult to believe that a 5-percent increase in length would have been a sufficient incentive for the filing down (or recasting) of all the type to be used.

Be that as it may, the overall magnitude of the opera-tion of producing the 42-line Bible was staggering. The amount of type alone would have required an immense effort of design and production. There are well over 2,-000 characters on each page, representing a font con-taining 290 different letters and symbols. To design, cut, and cast enough type to print only one page at a time would have been a major effort—but there is evidence to show that, even from the beginning, two presses were used, and this number was eventually increased to six. Six presses at a time, 2,000 pieces of type for each press (assuming one page at a time), and a comparable amount of type needed to set up new forms while the presses were at work!

It has been estimated that this edition ran to 210 copies: 180 printed on paper, and about 30 on vellum. To print 30 copies on vellum would have required more than 5,000 carefully prepared calfskins. Obviously, Gutenberg and Fust must have had high hopes for the financial success of this undertaking.

Then, suddenly and without apparent warning, John Fust brought suit against Gutenberg for the return of all the money which had been loaned or advanced to him— plus interest. This came to about 2,000 guldens, a sum so staggering that Gutenberg could never hope to pay even the interest. He had been living from hand to mouth for years, and in the year or so before the suit was filed, he had been devoting all of his time to the printing of the still-unfinished Bible. He had no source of income outside of the printing shop, and one can only assume that Fust was aware of this fact.

There are two theories which have been put forth by printing historians to explain Fust's motivation. The one most commonly held characterizes Fust as a practical and enterprising merchant who was well aware of the value of both Gutenberg's invention and of the potential market value of the work in progress. This theory would have Fust biding his time until he was certain that the work could be carried on without Gutenberg, and then, using his claim to title on the equipment, stepping in to take over the business.

The other theory would not paint Fust as quite such a grasping and unprincipled man. Fust, after all, had been putting money into the business for five years, without

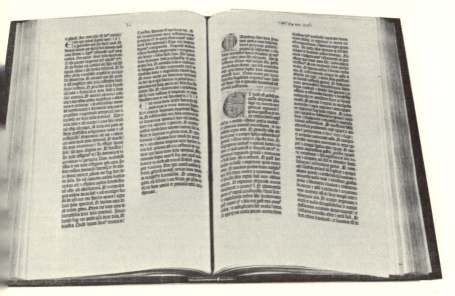

The Gutenberg Bible, first book printed from movable type. (New York Public Library)

any tangible return. He himself had borrowed money to support this enterprise, and his own interest payments were becoming an annoying reminder of the painfully slow progress. Gutenberg, the perfectionist, would not be hurried. Fust, the businessman, was impatient to see some sort of profit.

But whatever the reason—greed or natural concern for his investment—Fust took Gutenberg to court. There was some argument about the exact amounts of money involved, but in the end the court found for Fust and ordered that Gutenberg should repay all of the first 800 guldens, plus the portion of the second 800 guldens which had not properly been used "for the profit of both," with appropriate interest.

The record of this lawsuit, like so many of the records of Gutenberg's life, has not been preserved. However, once again thanks to the cumbersome legal machinery

of the day which required that a running summary be
made up at each step in any judicial proceeding, a brief
narrative of the trial has survived. In this it was noted
that the final action of the court was contingent upon
Fust carrying out one final, formal act: He must appear
at a local monastery and swear before God that he had,
in fact, been paying interest on some of the money
which he had advanced to Gutenberg. Fust appeared at
the appointed spot on the appointed day; Gutenberg
failed to show up, and in his stead sent two friends. Fust
took the oath; the verdict of the court was at that moment executed, and John Fust was now in the printing
business.

Fust did not delay in taking over the printing plant
and entered into an immediate partnership with Gutenberg's prime assistant, Peter Schoeffer. Schoeffer was an
artist and designer who had worked in Paris as an illu-
minator, as a scribe, and as a manuscript dealer. Fust, as
the businessman, handled the outside details and the
finances. The two made a good team and the firm of
Fust and Schoeffer became, for a time, the most important printing business in the world.

Their first joint venture was to complete the work on
the 42-line Bible. Quite possibly, most of the presswork
had already been finished and all that remained was to
organize the binding, distribution, and sale of the books.
There is some evidence for this, as one copy in existence
today bears a marginal notation that it had been rubri-
cated and bound in 1456.

The sale of the books was apparently successful, as
the partnership quickly moved ahead with other projects. Also, Peter Schoeffer married Fust's daughter and

started a dynasty of printers which was to last for about one hundred years.

Gutenberg himself drifted into bankruptcy. He was by no means finished with the business of printing, but without income and without funds, he was unable to keep up the interest payments on the "annuity" he had sold to Saint Thomas Paris in Strasbourg in 1442. The records of the parish show that he fell into default about 1457. Attempts to collect interest or principal from either Gutenberg or the man who had co-signed his note failed.

CHAPTER ELEVEN

Printing in the Marketplace

Why had Gutenberg been a relative failure, while Fust and Schoeffer apparently enjoyed immediate and continuing success? Surely not because they were better technicians, nor more imaginative, nor even necessarily better businessmen. Gutenberg, after all, had proven himself and his business acumen in a number of endeavors. The problem would seem to come to this: Gutenberg was running a heartbeat ahead of his times.

If the first problem which faced these early printers centered on the design and development of the purely mechanical systems and subsystems which make up the craft of printing, then the next problem was to find a market for the product. If there was no one who wished to buy a printed book, it did not matter how ingeniously it was done or how novel or how amazingly accurate a copy of the original text it may have been. If there was no one to buy, then there could be no sales, no profit and, essentially, little purpose to continue.

Books, even then, were nothing new to the world. There have been books of one sort or another as long as there has been writing. Through the centuries, with the perfection of various materials upon which writings could be preserved, the business of making and selling books became a well-organized operation. Well-organized, that is, by medieval standards—but not at all ineffective even in comparison with some of the undertakings of modern business.

While the earliest books survive from the days of the clay tablet and the papyrus roll, we can pick up the bookmaking story at about the end of the thirteenth century, for it was at this time that the first craft guilds, connected with books, were organized. It is also approximately at this time that paper (a Chinese invention, carried to Europe by Arab marauders) began to appear.

Until this time, most of the copying of texts took place in various monasteries scattered throughout the civilized world. In fact, it is to these monasteries that we are generally indebted for the preservation of any written materials at all—even for the very skill of committing language to a written form. When the barbarian hordes had swept over Europe, leaving death and destruction wherever they went, civilized man was plunged into the abyss of the Dark Ages. For several centuries, the most important, all-consuming activity of man became self-preservation. Formal education, as practiced under Roman rule, ceased; most men forgot that such a thing had ever existed. Except in the monasteries, where life went on in some isolation from the outside world, a small lamp of learning was kept lighted. It was in the monasteries that the first rudiments of the medieval school system were born and nurtured.

And it was also in the monasteries that some of the

precious manuscripts of the ancient authors were hidden from the vandals, safe from the weather, often forgotten—but preserved. When mankind began to awaken from the long sleep of ignorance—to awaken with a parched mind and a thirst for knowledge—it was from the monasteries that the first relief was to come. The monastic scribes, slowly and carefully and with reverence for the materials with which they worked, copied the texts of Bibles and prayer books and basic school lessons onto sheets of parchment. As years went by, more and more copies were made, and eventually copies became available for use outside the monastery walls. As the supply increased, so did the demand, and soon there were independent businessmen outside the monastic orders who were engaged in the trade of bookmaking.

These men organized their own guild and their own methods of production as well. It was not long before a number of assembly-line book factories appeared, in which a man trained in a particular skill would devote all of his effort to one facet of the bookmaking operation. One man might copy the text with a neat, artistic hand; another would draw in the large capital letters; still another would apply the gold ornamentation. Two other men would check the copy against the original, to ensure accuracy. Another team would handle the binding of the book—organizing the pages in serial order, sewing them together, making the "case" of leather and boards (often elaborately decorated), and fixing the text in the case. Some of the more active book factories sought a competitive edge by sending copyists out into distant lands, searching the monastic libraries for previously unpublished materials.

This work, while well organized, was by no means simple. The labor was tedious, the production limited. The manufacture of an average fine book might require as much as 297 man-days. As one might expect, the price for such a book was high. In a cash sale, the average parchment book might cost the equivalent of $200–$250; in a barter, the seller of a book might get a farm or a large vineyard in exchange. The countess of Anjou once gave two hundred sheep, five measures of wheat, and five measures of barley for a book of homilies. A truly fine book, heavily illuminated with gold and colors, was practically worth its weight in gold. A price of 1,000 guldens was not uncommon for such a book.

As paper came into more general use, during the course of the fourteenth century and into the first decades of the fifteenth century, book production became somewhat less complicated and less costly. Paper was ideally suited for books which did not need to be especially beautiful or treated with exceptional reverence. Hand labor, though tedious, was plentiful. As a result, by the early years of the fifteenth century, there were quite a few relatively inexpensive books on the market, for use primarily by students. In 1418, in Germany, an "ABC" could be purchased for 1 groschen; a "Donatus" might cost 10 groschen. In terms of the cost of living, books were still expensive enough; in a day when a hen could be purchased for 1 pfennig and a pound of good beef cost 2 pfennigs, 10 groschen (about 90 pfennig) could put a strain on the family budget.

Because most books were so valuable, they were kept chained to the shelves in libraries, and the sale of a copy was often handled with as much formality as the trans-

An early paper mill. (*Library of Congress*)

fer of a piece of real estate. Books could be pawned and books could be rented. Book transactions were usually handled by a man who dealt in other commodities besides books. He may have been a peddler, a moneylender, a dealer in old clothes, a perfumer, a grocer, or a mercer. But he had international connections and could order and ship books back and forth across the Continent and could usually locate copies of specific texts on order from a client.

Some cities became known as centers of the book trade—particularly Venice, Florence, and Paris. In the latter city, the trade in books was more controlled than in most places and a booksellers' guild had been formed quite early to regulate the sale of manuscripts. In Paris, hucksters and peddlers were forbidden to deal in books. They were considered too ignorant to handle such valuable materials and to be incapable of recognizing fraudulent or grossly inaccurate copies. The professional bookmen, jealous of their reputation, were concerned with the quality of the materials which they marketed.

While this book trade flourished in most of Europe, there was no such organized machinery for the selling of books in Germany, and only a scanty market. Such books as were sold were generally offered at the great yearly fairs held in the major trade centers. And the customers were limited: There were fewer wealthy nobles in Germany in the fourteenth and fifteenth centuries than there were in either France or Italy (where men vied with each other as a matter of pride, in the collection of literary treasures), and few nobles who had been stirred by the spirit of the Renaissance. Those men wishing to buy a text on a particular subject would not

A fifteenth-century library showing books chained to shelves.
(New York Public Library)

look to the local merchants, but would send off to the recognized centers of learning for a book on that subject. These were the cities where the great specialized universities had grown, where the world experts in each field had gathered to form the faculty—in Padua for medicine, in Bologna for jurisprudence, in Paris for theology.

Germany was not without its own universities, and there was certainly a need for books for use by the teachers and students, but the German market was additionally limited by a long-standing practice in which the student would make his own copy, as the teacher read aloud from the text.

Thus, with a small market for books, it is not surprising that the local trade in books was small—and this was the situation in which Gutenberg found himself about the year 1450. He could not make much money in producing books which the students themselves could acquire for only the cost of a few copying materials. The price of the early editions which issued from his presses —such as the "Donatus"—would certainly have been competitive with the price of a manuscript copy, but with little demand he would not have been able to offset the high costs of his overhead. This was perhaps a major factor in his continuing financial difficulties.

Further, this may well have been a major factor in Gutenberg's decision to produce a relatively expensive, high-quality book which could appeal to a wealthy purchaser. For even in Germany, where there were few book collectors *per se*, there was always a steady demand for the most important of all books—the Bible. Gutenberg deliberately set out to produce an edition of

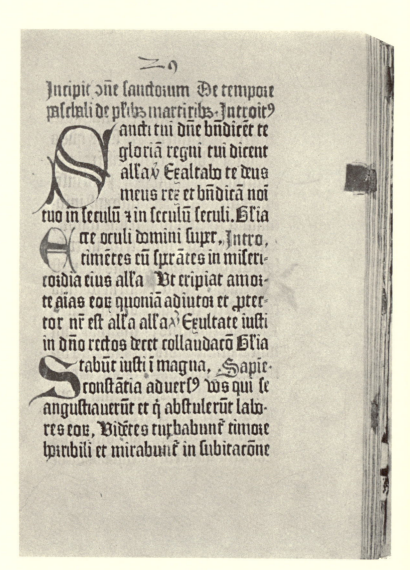

Page of a missal, probably printed by Gutenberg about 1450.
(New York Public Library)

the Bible which would have all the beauty and appeal of a carefully prepared manuscript edition. His would have one distinct commercial advantage, however—an exceptionally accurate and consistent text, at a cost reasonably below the current market. In this, Gutenberg succeeded, but he did not benefit from his success. The edition of the 42-line Bible was sold at a good profit—but a profit that went to the firm of Fust and Schoeffer.

Fust was astute enough not to try to limit the sale of books to the area around Mainz, and traveled extensively to promote business. There was, for many years, a pleasant myth about the travels and occupation of John Fust. Because of the novelty of his work—that is, because he was apparently able to produce any number of identical copies of a book—it was assumed by many people that he must have been in league with the devil. It is even probable that the professional copyists, seeing a definite threat to their own activities, made an effort to spread the tale in the hope that potential buyers would be frightened away.

CHAPTER TWELVE

The Final Years

After years of careful and unprofitable work, Johann Gutenberg, had come just to the brink of success—but he could go no further. There is little point in impugning the motives of John Fust without any tangible evidence; he had sufficient reasons for his foreclosure action simply to protect his rather sizable investment. He had, after all, been associated with Gutenberg for some five years, during which period there was little if any income to offset the great expenses involved in setting up a functional and operational printing business.

And yet, one might well wonder why he did not wait for just a few more months, until the great Bible should be completed. But this was a matter between Fust and Gutenberg, and Fust obviously was able to demonstrate, to the satisfaction of a judicial proceeding, that his action was legal.

Thus, for whatever reason, Gutenberg was faced with the prospect of starting his lifework over again. At least this time he was not starting from scratch. The research, the development, the design and perfection of equip-

ment and techniques had all been successfully completed. His schemes were no longer mere theory, but
were demonstrably practical. He had produced finished
copies of books which could be held in the hand. He
was without capital and equipment, but his knowledge
of his art and craft was still almost exclusively his own,
and the only printers then at work, anywhere, were
those who had learned the business from him. He may
have been penniless; he may have been down; he may
have been knocked into a daze by this catastrophic
blow to his ego. He may have been almost sixty years
old. But whatever he was, he was Gutenberg, a man
who had started many things at many different times of
his life. He was not ready to give up.

It was not long before he had located another financial backer—Dr. Konrad Humery, a citizen of Mainz,
who had sufficient faith in the inventor's abilities to advance money for the establishment of a printing shop, in
exchange for a pledge of the equipment as security.

Within two years, Gutenberg had built a new press,
designed and cast a new font of type, and issued a new
edition of the Bible.

This edition, called the 36-line Bible, is perhaps more
properly identified as "the Gutenberg Bible" than the
42-line issue because it may have been entirely his own
work. For many years, the 36-line Bible was something
of a bibliographic enigma. Some scholars presumed that
it must have preceded the 42-line edition because the
typeface is less refined and would seem to be earlier in
design and execution. However, certain errors which
appear in the text could only have resulted from the use
of a 42-line Bible as a master copy, which would ob-

viously make the 36-line Bible the later work. The cru-
dity of the typeface can be attributed to mechanical factors aggravated by a feeling of urgency in that there
could be no luxury of refinement and polish. A new
investor would have to be satisfied that reasonable progress was being made.

When first discovered, the 36-line Bible was attributed to a printer named Pfister, who established a shop
in the city of Bamberg sometime after 1460. This attri-
bution was logical, since Pfister worked with the same
font of type used in the printing of the 36-line edition;
however, the quality of the presswork on this Bible ex-
ceeds that of any work definitely known to have been
produced by the Bamberg printer. Most likely, Pfister
bought his type from Gutenberg, who would have been
happy to sell a substandard font once it had been replaced with something more to his taste. As it is with so
many things connected with the life and work of Johann
Gutenberg, this must be considered as judicious speculation rather than established fact; and, because of the
uncertainty surrounding the production of this edition,
the 36-line Bible has been variously known as the Pfister
Bible, the Bamberg Bible, and the Schelhorn Bible
(after the man who first discovered a copy). There are
only some fourteen copies of this work in existence
today, making it even rarer than the 42-line edition.

In the next few years (1457–60), Gutenberg was very
much at work as a printer (and as a teacher of printers,
staffing his shop with eager and talented apprentices at
least one of whom, Nicholas Jenson, had come from as
far away as Paris to study with Gutenberg). He produced several notable works, including a "Treatise on

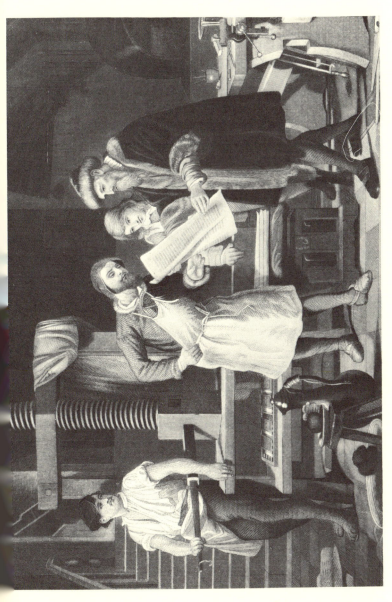

A painting by C. Pelton showing Johann Gutenberg reading a proof sheet fresh off the press. (Charles Phelps Cushing)

the Assumption of the Body of Our Lord" and a *summa* of Saint Thomas Aquinas. In 1460, he issued an ambitious theological dictionary, the "Catholicon," based on a thirteenth-century text. This edition contains an interesting and significant statement by the printer himself, presented as a colophon:

> By the help of the most High, at Whose will the tongues of infants become eloquent, and who ofttimes reveals to the lowly that which he hides from the wise, this noble work, Catholicon, in the year of the Lord's incarnation, 1460, in the bounteous city of Mainz of the renowned German nation, which the clemency of God has deigned with so lofty a light of genius and great gift prefer and render illustrious above all other nations of the earth, without help of reed, stylus or pen, by the wondrous agreement, proportion and harmony of punches and types, has been printed and brought to an end.

This is the last work which has been definitely attributed to Gutenberg, but his "presence" was to become known, on a worldwide scale, within a few years. In October, 1462, a relatively unimportant political skirmish incidentally resulted in an event of far-reaching consequence.

Some of the temporal and ecclesiastical princes of Germany became involved in a struggle for power—a struggle which was not limited to verbal wrangling but which erupted in a full-scale local war. Eight hundred horsemen and several thousand infantrymen, under the command of Adolph of Nassau, descended upon Mainz.

To set an "example" for the citizens, Adolph turned the town over to his soldiers for plunder and looting, bringing all commerce to a halt. With some warning from neighboring towns which had fallen to Adolph's ill-disciplined troops, the merchants of Mainz packed what they could on wagons and carts, and fled. The growing clan of printers, Gutenberg among them, were scattered into the countryside carrying whatever equipment they could salvage.

At first, it seemed as if another disaster had befallen the infant printing industry and its now aging founder. But the invasion proved to be more a catalyst than a poison, and the printers, flying like seeds in the wind, came to light on fertile ground wherever they went. Gutenberg had only gone a few miles, to the outlying village of Eltville, and soon returned to Mainz. But others had gone farther, and where they stopped, they found a ready market for their services. Several printers reached Strasbourg; at least one soon moved on to Cologne. Within two years, when word reached Italy of the marvelous new invention which was spreading through Germany, a team of printers was contacted and invited to move south to introduce their craft.

The sacking of Mainz by Adolph and his troops directly provoked the growth and spread of the printing industry at an unbelievable rate. By 1463, the selling price of a printed Bible was as low as one-tenth that of a manuscript copy, and the market seemed insatiable. By 1470, the Nuremburg printer Anthony Coburger could boast of 24 presses and 100 apprentices. By 1487, printing presses were at work in almost every European country, and before 1500, the number of active printers

in Europe had grown to more than 1,000. The number
of known editions of books published in the major centers of printing, before the year 1500, exceed 7,000—and
each edition comprised between 300 and 1,000 copies.
Even today, almost 30,000 copies of pre-1500 books remain. These are collectively referred to as an *incunabula*,
from the Latin, meaning, literally, "in the cradle."

And what of Johann Gutenberg? He returned to
Mainz and apparently continued with his printing activities, although no particular work from this period has
been identified as his. His fortunes seem to have continued on the decline even as his reputation grew. On Jan-
uary 17, 1465, the archbishop of Mainz appointed Gutenberg, "on account of his grateful and willing service,
his servant and courtier for life, promising to supply him
with clothing and each year 20 malter of corn and 2
fuder of wine." The particular "service" was not enu-
merated, but this appointment may have been by way of
reward to the elderly and destitute inventor who had
brought such glory to Mainz.

The best available information indicates that Gutenberg died early in 1468. In February of that year, his
last patron, Dr. Humery, requested that the printing
equipments which had belonged to the late Gutenberg
be given to him because, in the terms of their financial
agreement, these items should now properly be regarded as his rightful property. The archbishop agreed
that Dr. Humery could have the equipments—but with
two conditions: one, that they not be removed from
Mainz by Dr. Humery; and, two, that if they were to be
sold, a citizen of Mainz should be given first considera-
tion before they could be offered to outsiders.

Gutenberg's death may actually have occurred on the third of February. This is suggested by one of those casual footnotes to history which from time to time are brought to light by careful research. A bit of writing on the flyleaf of a book which once belonged to a priest in Mainz offers the information that "the honorable master Henne Ginssfleiss" died February 3, 1468. This cannot be accepted as definitive evidence, in that so many members of the Gensfleisch family lived in and around Mainz and any number of these might have been named John. Because of this, scholars of printing history are generally very careful in crediting any such evidence unless Gutenberg is in fact identified with the use of his usual name. But in this particular instance, as one historian has pointed out, this notation need not be completely ignored as it seems unlikely that any other John Gensfleisch would have been given the doubly respectful title of "the honorable master."

CHAPTER THIRTEEN

The Myth of the "Other" Inventor

The name Johann Gutenberg—or any variation thereof —does not appear on the title page or in the colophon of any book or printed work which may be attributed to his press. The often fragmentary legal and court records, which comprise the entire body of documentary material about Gutenberg, frequently contain no reference to printing or to any related procedure, and several of the earlier direct references to printing are sufficiently ambiguous that they may be considered to be open to "interpretation," when one is trying to establish a period during which Gutenberg actually began work as a printer.

There has never been any significant doubt that he was, in fact, a printer. The records of the Fust suit, and the request by Dr. Humery for the return of printing equipments, provide sufficient substantiation. The principal issue, when joined by disputatious historians, has revolved around the possibility that someone other than Gutenberg was the inventor of printing.

Many serious and otherwise conscientious scholars

spent many years searching for a rationale which would permit them to discount any evidence which pointed to Gutenberg as the inventor. This is a curious approach to scholarly research and seems to have resulted from motives fostered by something less than a dispassionate interest in the "truth." As noted earlier, much of the anti-Gutenberg activity was inspired by strong feelings of nationalistic fervor—*i.e.*, should credit for the invention of printing be given to Mainz, Germany; or to Strasbourg, France; or Avignon; or Paris; or to the Dutch city of Haarlem? Other historians took sides only because of their own professional rivalries. And still others, finding what seemed to be valid clues pointing to other inventors, evolved elaborate and sometimes quite fanciful theories with which they soon became hopelessly enamored.

There are definite bits of evidence surviving from the early fifteenth century which demonstrate that some men somewhere—other than Gutenberg and elsewhere than Mainz—were involved in typographic development. But it is difficult—if not impossible—to accurately date and place these materials, and therefore most of them must remain as typographic curiosities. Yet the efforts of two men, exemplified by some of these historic bits, merit brief attention. One of these men worked in France, and the other in Holland. The work of the latter has provoked an elegant myth which must be examined in some detail as it shows up at the center of most efforts to discredit Gutenberg.

The existence of the Frenchman is known through some interesting but inconclusive early references to printing materials which occur in a few contracts and

receipts discovered recently in an ancient archive.
These note that a goldsmith named Procopius Waldfoghel was involved in the production of "alphabets of
steel," using various metals such as tin, lead, brass, iron,
and steel, which would indicate that punches, matrices,
and cast letters may have been part of his operation. No
sample of printing from these "alphabets" has been
identified, and some scholars speculate that Waldfoghel
was not so much a printer as he may have been an early
typefounder, attempting to make and sell a product for
the use of others who would do the actual printing. He
began his work in Avignon, not far from Strasbourg, at
just about the time that Gutenberg returned from that
city to Mainz probably in 1444.

Because of the proximity of place and time, the
suggestion has been advanced that the materials with
which he worked may have been among those stolen
from the room of Andrew Dritzehen, following that
partner's death. It has also been suggested that Gutenberg himself may have been involved in some sort of
business venture with the goldsmith. More likely is the
theory that Waldfoghel had worked with the goldsmith
who supplied Gutenberg in Strasbourg and from this association had gained some knowledge of the processes
involved and sought to set out on his own. He does not
seem to have enjoyed much success. The testimony of
one of his customers noted that his procedure "is practical if one applies oneself diligently." Apparently there
was not enough diligence in Avignon; the name of Procopius Waldfoghel quickly disappears into the mists of
history.

The Dutch printer was definitely involved in the pro-

duction of finished typographic printing, probably contemporaneous with Gutenberg's earliest efforts and possibly even somewhat before. He has never been
identified and is generally referred to as the "unknown
Dutch printer." Numerous undated parchment fragments of his work have been discovered, many of them
having been used as part of the bindings of manuscript
books of the middle fifteenth century. Some of these
fragments contain only a line or two of printing, while
others embody entire pages. The Dutch printer issued
such works as a "Donatus," an "ABC," and a *Speculum
Humanae Salvationis* ("Mirror of Human Salvation"),
using type fonts with as many as 188 characters. Certain
technical features of these fonts and of the presswork
tend to indicate that the printer was experiencing some
difficulty in his work, and that he probably needed a
fresh developmental effort to achieve a more practical
system. Available evidence seems to demonstrate that
the Dutch printer was not succeeded in his work by any
other printer, and that quite possibly he died before he
was able to improve his technical proficiency.

There is always the possibility that Gutenberg might
have seen some of the work of this man and may have
been thereby inspired to begin his own efforts—and vice
versa. However, no connection between the two printers can be demonstrated, and only one definite conclu-
sion can be drawn: The efforts of the Dutch printer did
not bear fruit and remained as an isolated experience,
while the work of Gutenberg was to lead, directly and
specifically, to the development, perfection, and dissem-
ination of the art and craft of printing.

It was upon the work of the unknown Dutch printer

that the anti-Gutenberg faction were to base most of their theories. In this, they were substantially aided by a late-sixteenth-century account describing the invention of printing, in Haarlem, by one Laurens Janszoon Coster. This account appeared in a book written in 1568 by Hadrianus Junius, entitled *Batavia*. This was a "history" of Holland.

The term "history" is here applied in a most casual sense, for Junius' sense of history itself seems to have been quite casual. Whatever the merits of the material about Coster, the book was hardly complete or even partially accurate. The author, perhaps in an attempt to make his book as interesting as possible to the average reader, included a great deal of demonstrably fanciful material. For example, Junius noted that a certain noblewoman had given birth to 365 children. This incredible happening was attributed to the fact that the woman had been the victim of a gypsy's curse, by which it was decreed that she would have as many children as there were days in the year. (Modern authors have researched this incident and discovered that the woman did exist and had, in fact, been placed under a gypsy curse—but that the curse had been delivered two days before the end of the year, and that the lady subsequently gave birth to twins.)

Junius devoted five pages of *Batavia* to the story of Coster, and in them he unfolded a marvelously romantic tale. Coster, an elderly man much devoted to his grandchildren, went for a walk in the woods one day and hit upon the idea of making some interesting novelties for them, by carving letters of the alphabet on birch bark. By then pressing the piece of bark, smeared with some ink, against a piece of paper, the children would be able to produce a few lines of writing. Following this initial experiment, Coster was struck by true inspiration: If he were somehow to separate and move the letters, and make them of a durable material like metal, he would be able to produce entire books of printing.

He set to work at once, designing and building his equipments and soon was producing finished work. Then, just as he was about to achieve real success, catastrophe struck: On Christmas night, a wicked servant betrayed him, stole all his equipment, and fled to Germany. The servant soon appeared in Mainz, using the stolen equipment. Coster, heartbroken at this treachery and dismayed by the loss of years of hard work, never recovered from the shock and never printed another line.

(It is interesting to note that other variations of this tale have shown up through the years, with John Fust in Mainz being the inventor and Gutenberg his unfaithful servant who ran off to Strasbourg with the materials; or, in a version published in Strasbourg in 1536, the inventor was Hans Metlin and "through infidelity" his art was wrongfully taken to Mainz. A Dutch version, circa 1628, named Coster's servant as Johann Gutenberg himself.)

As with the story of the prolific noblewoman, Junius did not invent this episode but merely transcribed an existing bit of folklore. For this, he based his information on an interview with his tutor, Nicholas Galius, who recalled a childhood conversation with an eighty-year-old bookbinder named Cornelius, in which that elderly fellow described his own work in Coster's shop. This rather tenuous data (which, by the time it was committed to writing, was 128 years removed from the incident in question) became the entire foundation for a voluminous literature about Coster. Much of the volume can be attributed to one man, Jan Hendrick Hessels. He was a native of Haarlem, who spent most of his life attempting to prove that Gutenberg had nothing whatever to do with the invention of printing. He wrote no fewer than four major books on this subject (including such provocative titles as *Haarlem the Birthplace of Printing, Not Mentz* and *The Gutenberg Fiction*) and authored related articles for three succeeding editions of the *Encyclopedia Britannica* (9th ed, 1888; 10th ed, 1902; and 11th ed, 1912). His firmly stated position was that "we have no choice but to say that the invention of printing with moveable types took place at Haarlem about the year 1445 by Laurens Janszoon Coster."

All efforts by less biased researchers to substantiate this theory have failed. No contemporary mention exists in any form referring to any sort of printing. There were two men living in Haarlem during the general period in question who bore the names Laurens Janszoon and Laurens Janszoon Coster, but one of them died long before 1445 and the other was too young to have had any grandchildren at that time. A Dutch historian has discovered a record dated 1474 which notes that there was, indeed, a bookbinder named Cornelius who lived in Haarlem in that year. However, if Coster had progressed in his work to the point where he needed the services of a bookbinder, it would seem that some knowledge of his efforts would have been common in Haarlem. It would also seem unlikely that he would have given up, "heartbroken" over the loss of his type fonts.

There are many other reasons for not giving much credence to the tale of Coster. Early printed books which referred to printing in Holland never mention his name, and one early Dutch book specifically credited Gutenberg with the invention. When typographic printing was introduced into Haarlem in 1483 by a transient printer, no one—not even Cornelius the bookbinder—came forth to claim this as a local invention. If there had been a carefully preserved legend about this matter, it should probably have become a matter of wider knowledge in a shorter period of time than 128 years.

Junius himself dates Coster's invention at 1440, which was at least four years after Gutenberg had begun work with printing. There have been several attributions of an earlier date for Coster, but most of these are pure fancy or are based upon "dated" forgeries planted by overzealous supporters. But it was not difficult for an eager historian to fall for such deception. In the mid-nineteenth century, H. N. Humphries wrote of the unknown Dutch printer's edition of *Speculum*: "The evidence that it was the work of Coster, and that it was produced not later than 1430, or about 20 years earlier than the Bible of Gutenberg, is, I understand, now accepted by the best authorities as practically conclusive."

Incidentally, one "expert" engaged in some interesting scholarly juggling to demonstrate that references to the making of mirrors (in Latin, *speculum*) which appear in the Strasbourg documents of 1439, were in fact carefully disguised references to the production of the book *Speculum* in which Gutenberg, with the aid of Coster's treacherous servant, would have then been involved. (In point of fact, no edition of *Speculum* has ever been attributed to Gutenberg.) In this same

connection, Hessels took another tack and completely
dismissed the whole idea that the Strasbourg documents
had any reference whatever to printing. Writing for the
Encyclopedia Britannica, he volunteered the unsup-
ported claim that "in former years . . . the records of
the Strasbourg lawsuit of 1439 . . . were considered to
prove the invention of printing at Strasbourg . . . by
Gutenberg. However, nobody would now assert that
printing was invented in 1439 or at Strasbourg; and
those who still believe that Gutenberg was the inventor
of printing refer to them only as showing that he was a
mechanic as early as 1439, and that he understood the
art of pressing."

Perhaps the most significant reason for discounting
the Coster myth is that the type fonts used by Gutenberg are all distinctly different from those used by the
unknown Dutch printer. If Gutenberg had received a
quantity of stolen type—supposedly the entire stock of
Coster's shop—it is improbable that he would have gone
to the trouble and expense of designing and producing a
completely new set.

And even more to the point in establishing Gutenberg's claim is the evidence offered by his own contemporaries. The generally accepted tradition that Johann
Gutenberg was the inventor of printing has been
strengthened through the years by the discovery of a
number of written and printed references to the man
and his work. These firmly place Mainz as the center of
early printing activity and just as firmly establish that
Gutenberg was the principal figure in that activity.

Indeed, Gutenberg's reputation was no secret in his
own town. A letter written in 1470 by a Frenchman de-

scribes a visit to Mainz and notes that "they tell us that there, not far from the city of Mainz, the art of printing was first of all invented by one John, whose surname was Gutenberg."

Another letter, written in the same year by a French scholar, was somewhat more flowery but nonetheless specific:

> There has been discovered in Germany a wonderful new method for the production of books, and those who have mastered this method are taking their invention from Mainz out into the world somewhat as the old Grecian warriors took their weapons from the belly of the Trojan horse. The light of this wonderful discovery will spread from Germany to all parts of the earth. I have been told . . . that Gutenberg has succeeded in producing books by means of metal letters in place of using the handiwork of the scribes. . . . [bringing] more blessings upon the world that were given by the goddess Ceres, for Ceres could only bestow material food, while through Gutenberg the productions of the thinkers could be brought within the reach of all the people.

In Rome, in 1474, due credit was given to Gutenberg in a chronicle which states, "Jacobus, surnamed Gutenberg, a native of Strasbourg, and a certain other whose name was Fust, having obtained skill in making impressions of letters upon parchment by means of metal types, became known at Mainz, a city of Germany, as the printers each of 300 leaves a day."

And John Schoeffer, son of Peter and grandson of John Fust, added a dedication at the end of an edition of Livy which he issued in 1505:

> May your majesty deign to accept this book which was printed at Mainz, the town in which the admirable art of typography was invented, in the year 1450, by John Gutenberg, and afterwards brought to perfection at the expense, and by the labor of, John Fust and Peter Schoeffer.

Epilogue

This then is the story of Johann Gutenberg. It is a story concerning one of the most important men of all times, and yet a story of shadows, of unanswered questions, of scholarly speculation. A story in which virtually the only facts are provided by legal records which tend more to document his failures than his successes.

Nevertheless, the doubts that persist are doubts about the man, not about his achievement. Johann Gutenberg provided mankind with what may well be the most significant single tool ever invented—the tool whereby the thoughts, hopes, anxieties, and ideas of men may be communicated through all time.

While the nature of printing has changed over the centuries, Gutenberg's basic techniques persisted for a remarkable span of four hundred years before falling to the advances of the industrial revolution. These advances have held for about one hundred years, and now they too are to be superseded by new techniques, even new concepts. Letterpress printing with cast type is giving way to offset printing with photographic typesetting; even the common ground of both is being invaded by computers and cathode ray tubes. With the printed word, language became fixed—the English of today is still very close to the English of Chaucer's south-of-London. With television, the spoken language is more plastic and a new visual language of rapidly changing images is evolving. "Nonlinear communication" is the rallying cry of a new breed of language specialists. But the printed word is still with us and will continue to be for countless years to come.

Requiescat in pace, Johann Gutenberg.

Printing: The First Fifty Years

The most successful of the early printers kept a sharp eye on the market potential for their efforts and gave the public what it wanted. This naturally varied from country to country: In Italy, birthplace of the Renaissance, there was a steady demand for copies of the pagan (Greek and Roman) classics, while in Germany, theological works and common folk literature sold well, but the buyers of books were not yet ready for Greek pastorales.

As more and more printed works began to reach the public, the market for manuscript books began to deteriorate—much to the consternation of the professional scribes and much to the horror of the wealthy nobles who had spent fortunes in compiling collections of expensive hand-copied books. In a vain effort to protect their livelihood, the scribes of Genoa in 1474 petitioned the senate for expulsion of all printers from that city. The request was ignored. The profession of scribe did not immediately disappear, however, as many of the more conservative scholars and collectors felt that

"cheap" printed books were suited only to the requirements of the vulgar lower classes.

The great manuscript dealer Vespasiano, writing in
1482 about the Ducal library in Urbino, proclaimed, "In
this library all the volumes are of perfect beauty, all
written by skilled scribes on parchment and many of
them adorned with exquisite miniatures. The collection
contains no single printed book. The Duke would be
ashamed to have a printed book in his library." Also de-
fending manuscript books, an abbot wrote (sometime
before 1494), "A work written on parchment could be
preserved for a thousand years, while it is probable that
no volume printed on paper will last for more than two
centuries. Many important works have not been printed,
and the copies required of these must be prepared by
scribes. The scribe who ceases his work because of the
invention of the printing-press can be no true lover of
books, in that, regarding only the present, he gives no
due thought to the intellectual cultivation of his succes-
sors. The printer has no care for the beauty and the artistic form of his books, while with the scribe this is a
labor of love."

The scribes managed to keep going, in some fashion,
and some of them, in following their labor of love, discovered that the printers actually made things easier for
them by providing legible, easily copied texts. Working
with an intelligence more mechanical than that of the
machines they so feared, these scribes followed printed
texts with such faithfulness that they even included,
carefully hand-drawn, the imprint of the printer.

But the fate of the scribes became abundantly clear as
the prices of printed books steadily declined. Even the

earliest printers were able to produce a copy of a book to sell for one-fifth the price of a comparable manuscript text, and before the beginning of the sixteenth century a reader could buy one hundred printed copies for the price of the same text, hand-copied, fifty years earlier. The more enlightened managers of the manuscript production factories soon switched over to printing. The Brothers of the Common Life, who for years had specialized in manuscript copies of "popular" books, were operating no fewer than sixty different printing plants by 1490.

The printers did not exactly have a smooth and quick road to success, but at least they were not doomed by obsolescence. They were prey to piracy; victims of strikes (the first recorded was a compositors' strike in 1471); harassed by temperamental authors; subject to censorship and control by church and state. (Printers and publishers are still bothered by these same problems, after more than five hundred years. Some things never change.)

The whole concept of "literary property" began to evolve, and with it the protection of copyright laws and agreements, after printers watched their finest and most ambitious works being pirated and sold in cheap facsimile. In many cases, the material was legally "in the public domain" but when a printer had put a great deal of time and effort into locating a previously unprinted work and in preparing it for the press, he would be rightfully distressed to see a fly-by-night transient printer simply duplicate the book and sell it for a fraction of the price which he must charge.

Authors of original material were also victims of literary piracy, but their early concern seems not to have been so much over the loss of any possible revenues— payment by a publisher to an author was a rare thing no matter how legitimate the venture—but rather at the pain in seeing their works mutilated by careless and unsupervised production. The Dutch humanist scholar Erasmus (1466–1536), perhaps thus stung by the theft of some of his own writings, noted complainingly: "A dealer who sells English stuffs under the guise of Venetian is punished, but the printer who in place of correct texts, misleads and abuses the reader with pages the contents of which are an actual trial and torment, escapes unharmed. . . . The authorities will supervise with arbitrary regulations the proper methods for the baking of bread, but concern themselves not at all as to the correctness of the work of the printers, although the influence of bad typography is far more injurious than that of bad bread."

Authors had difficulties enough with their regular publishers. If any writer of today wished to compile a record of author/publisher disputes and differences of opinion—a record, to be sure, which could fill a good-sized library—one of his early entries would be some correspondence between an author and his publisher in 1525. The author thought the production was going much too slowly, and he did not like the illustrations (the publisher was using Italian artists; the author would have preferred "good Germans"). As the delays mounted, so did the author's frustration and he wrote that, if he could have foreseen all the difficulties in advance, he would have burned the manuscript rather than turn it over to be printed. The publisher, in rebuttal, maintained that the manuscript was ill prepared by the author and that the compositors had been experiencing a most difficult time in following the text.

The printers early learned of another problem—one that is still very much a part of the business. That is, that a printshop is both an interesting place to visit and a fine atmosphere in which a "customer" might work out his fantasies that he will someday bring forth a momentous project in which the printer may have a share. The Italian printer Aldus Manutius (1450–1515) was constantly bothered by "heedless visitors who use up my office hours to no purpose." He made so bold as to have a large sign put on his door, advising, "Whoever thou art, thou art earnestly requested by Aldus, to state thy business briefly and take thy departure promptly. In this way thou mayest be of service even as was Hercules to the weary Atlas. For this is a place of work for all who may enter."

The most serious continuing problem which rose to face the printers was that of censorship. On the face of it, censorship was intended as a "protection" for the people; but the core of the issue was—and always has been—who shall be the censor, who the judge of what is good or bad, right or wrong?

The major virtue of printing was not so much that it made inexpensive books available to everyone, but that it made books, therefore, available. Ideas, not paper and ink, were the true commodity of the printer, and the true impact of the invention of printing was not upon the commerce of the bookseller, but upon the minds of men. The spirit of the Renaissance burned through the Western world, carried along by books, tracts, pam-

phlets. There was a thirst for knowledge which was satisfied by the availability of good texts; and there was a
searching for a new condition for mankind, the ideals of
which were carried to the people by the printed word.
Previously, the wretched lower classes had accepted
their position but with new knowledge came new power.
The agitators ranged from anarchists who advocated
the "slaughter (of) the fattened herds which have
so long pastured their lusting hearts on the poverty of
the common man" to more temperate prophets who saw
true reform coming through less drastic action: men like
Erasmus, whose tract "Praise of Folly" (1509) attacked
fools—particularly ecclesiastical fools—in the wittiest
and most entertaining fashion and swiftly went through
twenty-seven editions; and men like Martin Luther, to
whom the printed word became a sword for the carving
of a new order out of religious chaos.

The Church had at first welcomed the introduction of
printing as "a gift directly from God himself" by means
of which "it will be possible to place in the hands of all
men treasures of literature and of knowledge which
have heretofore been out of reach." But too many men
had too much of a vested interest, in the Church, in a
business sense, to permit free and open criticism to cir-
culate among the people. These men responded to the
threat by forbidding the printing of any Protestant materials, and in some countries—particularly France—the
publishing of all writings other than accepted, approved
religious texts was forbidden. The "power of the press,"
however, was well enough established by this time so
that censorship could not hold back the progress of
ideas.

Bibliography

Accurate materials on the life and work of Gutenberg are scarce, often available only in specialized collections and frequently not available in English translation. The following bibliography lists those particular works which the author believes to be of more than passing interest and which can probably be located through normally operative library channels. This does not include general studies about life in the Middle Ages, of which any number of good examples may be found.

De Vinne, Theodore L. *The Invention of Printing.* New York, 1878. Written by a printer whose practical knowledge of the subject gave him an insight not always found in the works of professional scholars. In spite of the date, this book has held up well.

Encyclopaedia Britannica. 9th ed. New York, 1888. Article, *Typography,* by Hessels, J. H. A strong anti-Gutenberg bias in material offered as definitive. More recent editions have corrected this view.

Fuhrmann, Otto W. *Gutenberg and the Strasbourg*

Documents of 1439. New York, 1940. Reprints the text of the surviving documents, with a collation of the various translations. Also contains a good exploration of the known facts surrounding the mystery of the invention of printing.

Hessels, Jan Hendrik. *The Gutenberg Fiction.* London, 1912. Sets forth that author's contention that Gutenberg was not the inventor of printing.

Lehmann-Haupt, Hellmut. *Gutenberg and the Master of the Playing Cards.* New Haven and London, 1966. Theorizes a link between Gutenberg and the invention of copper engraving.

McMurtrie, Douglas C. *The Book: The Story of Printing and Bookmaking.* New York, 1937.

Tomlinson, Laurence. *Gutenberg and the Invention of Printing.* Washington, D.C., 1938.

COMMANDER BRAYTON HARRIS, a public relations specialist for the U.S. Navy, brings a unique background to the writing of Johann Gutenberg. Deeply interested in printing and graphic arts, he owned and operated a publishing and printing concern in San Francisco. A graduate of the University of Illinois, he is the author of two books and numerous articles.

Index